EXPLORING NEW TESTAMENT GREEK: A WAY IN

Peter Kevern
and
Paula Gooder

scm press

© Peter Kevern and Paula Gooder 2004

British Library Cataloguing in Publication data

A catalogue record for this book is available from the British Library

0 334 02942 2

First published in 2004 by SCM Press
9–17 St Albans Place, London N1 0NX

www.scm-canterburypress.co.uk

SCM Press is a division of
SCM-Canterbury Press Ltd

Printed and bound in Great Britain by
Biddles Ltd, www.biddles.co.uk

Contents

Introduction   1

1 Letters and Words   9
2 Finding Your Way Around a Sentence   24
3 Understanding How Greek Words Work   40
4 Introduction to Nouns and Their Endings   53
5 More Noun Endings and More Pronouns   71
6 Words that Describe   91
7 Simple Verbs   110
8 Tenses   134
9 Voice: Active, Passive and Middle   159
10 Participles and the Articular Infinitive   178
    Epilogue   200

Check List of Grammatical Words used in this Course   203
Appendix: Useful tables   209
Lexicon of Greek Words   228

Introduction

This book is designed to help anyone who wishes to enrich their understanding of the New Testament by looking at the Greek text. Whether you are a preacher, Bible student or simply someone who is interested in deepening your understanding of the text, this book will help you to gain some access to New Testament Greek. If you invest a reasonable amount of time and energy, you should quite quickly start to gain insights into how the language works and why such study is important when it comes to understanding the New Testament.

Although you may find it helpful to study in the company of others, the course in this book is designed so that you can work through it by yourself. In order to make the process of learning as simple and accessible as possible, we have limited the scope of the book to skills and information that are directly relevant to New Testament study. The idea is that you will develop a 'feel' for the way Greek works, learn how to use that knowledge in understanding New Testament texts and begin to appreciate how some of the richness of the original Greek text can be lost in the process of translation into English.

Inevitably, this means that we have had to leave out some of the things you may expect to find in a conventional language course. You will not find here many grammatical tables or long lists of Greek words to learn. You will not learn how to translate whole chapters of the Bible from Greek to English, or from English to Greek. If this book captures your interest and gives you a taste for language study, you may wish to go on and study a more comprehensive course in New Testament Greek. If you do, you should find the challenge has been made easier for having studied this book. But, if by the end of this book you feel you have as much understanding of New Testament Greek as you want or need, you will still have a valuable skill that will stand you in good stead as you study the Bible.

By the end of this course, you should be able to:

• Identify key Greek words and phrases, exploring for yourself their meaning, and where and how they are used in the New Testament.

• Translate short passages of the Greek New Testament with the help of an interlinear translation, dictionary and/or website.

• Understand observations about the Greek grammar of a passage such as you may encounter in a biblical commentary, using them to enrich your own understanding of the biblical text.

• Make your own observations about the grammar of a particular passage, drawing your own conclusions about the way it should be best understood.

• Understand why each English version of the New Testament can only represent some of the possible meanings of a passage, and decide for yourself which version gives the best translation.

HOW TO USE THIS BOOK

1 It helps if you can find a block of time (at least two hours) to work through each chapter. Get into the habit of reading a chapter several times before going on to the next one. Tackle the chapters in order, but be prepared to go back over material you did not understand first time around.

2 Rather than include all the materials you need in this volume (which would make it very long and difficult to use!) you will find that you are being directed to free-access websites where

you can find out the information on the Internet. For those who are not comfortable using the Internet, you will find the examples can just as easily be tackled using a Greek–English dictionary (technically known as a 'lexicon' though we shall use the word 'dictionary' throughout this book) and an interlinear Greek–English version of the New Testament.

To get the most out of this course of study you therefore need the following:

- A copy of the New Testament in English (the New Revised Standard Version is used here).

- **Either** access to the Internet for these sites:

  www.greekbible.com, http://bible.crosswalk.com and www.unbound.biola.edu.

- **Or** these books: a Greek–English dictionary and a Greek–English interlinear New Testament.

  The most helpful dictionaries are:

  Newman, B.M., *A Concise Greek–English Dictionary of the New Testament*, Stuttgart: United Bible Societies, 2000.
  Trenchard, W.C., *A Concise Dictionary of New Testament Greek*, Cambridge, Cambridge University Press, 2003.

  There are numerous interlinears of the New Testament based on different English translations of the Bible. One particularly good one is:

  Marshall, A., *The Interlinear NRSV–NIV Parallel New Testament in Greek and English*, Grand Rapids: Zondervan, 1994.

- Other resources you may find useful are:

  A concordance that refers to the Greek words underlying the English translation, such as:

  The Strongest Strong's Exhaustive Concordance, Grand Rapids: Zondervan, 2001. This includes a dictionary of Greek words too.

A book that goes through the Bible verse by verse, giving you the form (noun, verb, etc. of the word) and its meaning, such as:

> Rogers, C.L. Jr and Rogers C.L. III, *The New Linguistic and Exegetical Key to the Greek New Testament*, Grand Rapids: Zondervan, 1998.

If you are studying using the websites, you may still wish to purchase the books. In any case, they are a good investment for future biblical study.

3 The emphasis of this book is on practical skills that you can use in New Testament study. When a new idea is introduced in the text, there are some examples that you can do to reinforce what you have just learned enabling you to put it into practice. We recommend that you do the examples as you go along and check your answers, to build your confidence and to make sure that you have understood what you are doing. Sometimes, the answers are self-evident or can be checked against an English translation of the New Testament. Where this is not the case, you will find a number directs you to a note at the end of the chapter which gives you the answer.

If you want to explore a theme or practise a skill further, you will find additional information and examples on the website that accompanies this book:

www.queens.ac.uk/greek

GETTING STARTED

Using the Internet

If you are using the Internet, a good place to start is *The Greek New Testament Gateway*, at www.ntgateway.com/greek. As a gateway site, it doesn't carry much information itself, but has a lot of links to useful web pages elsewhere on the Internet. Two of the websites we will be using can be reached via this page: try clicking on the links to *The Online Greek Bible* and *The Unbound Bible*. A wide range of other resources are available on the Gateway, which is constantly being updated. We recommend you spend some time exploring it.

The other site used in this book is *Crosswalk* at http:// bible.crosswalk.com. This is particularly good for looking up words you don't know and finding out their meaning. However, in order to be able to read Greek on this site, you may need to download another font onto your computer, the BST font. To do this you can go to http://bible.crosswalk.com/OtherResources/ BSTFonts/ and click on the link for your sort of computer.

Using Books

If you are using books, you should have no trouble understanding the Greek dictionary. It is organized alphabetically just like an English dictionary, except that being in Greek it runs from A to Ω rather than from A to Z. The Greek–English interlinear shows a line of Greek text, and underneath each word is the English translation. Sometimes the Greek word has to be translated with two English ones, (which both appear under the Greek) and sometimes an extra word has to be supplied (in italics). Sometimes the word order is different, and little numbers by the English words indicate the order in which they need to be read. For example, this is the way John 7.6 looks in the version of the interlinear New Testament recommended above:

NRSV	NIV	Greek
Jesus said to them, "My time has not yet come, but your time is always here.	Therefore Jesus told them, "The right time for me has not yet come: for you any time is right	Λέγει οὖν αὐτοῖς ὁ Says therefore to them – Ἰησοῦς· ὁ καιρὸς ὁ ἐμὸς Jesus: *The* ²time – ¹my οὔπω πάρεστιν, ὁ δε καιρὸς ὁ not yet is arrived, but *the* ²time ὑμέτερος πάντοτε ἐστιν ἕτοιμος ¹your always is ready

NOTES FOR TUTORS AND COURSE ORGANIZERS

The material in this book was originally taught as a 10 credit module at Level 2 over one semester. It was taught in two 90 minute sessions each week. In the first session each week we talked through the material in a chapter, taking just one representative example of each point. The second session was a voluntary tutorial, primarily for reinforcement and student support: all students were expected to complete all the set examples, but those who chose could attend this second session and do so as part of a group. This pattern was adopted because of the limitations of the timetable rather than by conviction: an alternative would have been to work through a chapter more slowly, over two taught sessions.

Chapters are structured to allow the tutor to break off at any one of several points; there is no reason to insist on completing exactly one chapter in each week or session. This means that the course can be accommodated to different teaching styles and session lengths. Nevertheless, it is important to work through the material in the order given, since later work always assumes knowledge of earlier material.

Sample assessments based on our experience of teaching the module at Level 2 can be found on the website.

TEXTS USED AND ABBREVIATIONS

Most of the time, the English translation that we have drawn on in this book is the New Revised Standard Version (NRSV). However, as one of the aims in this course is to help you to compare translations and make decisions about which you prefer, we have, in places, used a number of other English versions. On such occasions, we have indicated this by putting the version used in brackets after the text. All translations marked with an asterisk are the authors' own.

Throughout the book we have used only one Greek text, Nestle–Aland's 27th edition of the Greek New Testament (NA27).

The English versions used and their abbreviations are as follows:

*	Authors' own translation
NRSV	New Revised Standard Version
KJV	King James Version
NKJV	New King James Version
NIV	New International Version
GNB	Good News Bible
NCV	New Century Version
NLB	New Living Bible
NAS	New American Standard

ACKNOWLEDGEMENTS

A number of people have contributed to the making of this book. Worthy of particular mention are the students of New Testament Greek at both Ripon College, Cuddesdon and the Queen's Foundation, Birmingham. Any programme of study is only of use if it is clear and comprehensible to the students themselves, and their insights and suggestions have made all the difference.

Special thanks also to Rachel Kevern, who began by reading the manuscript for obvious errors but found herself functioning as a copy-editor, and even rewriting sections of the text! The only reason this book is not littered with inaccuracies is because of her diligent work: any that remain are entirely the responsibility of the authors.

1

Letters and Words

All of us use quite a lot of Greek every day – without even knowing it! Most of the time we use it in technical terms, because for a long time it was fashionable for scientists and scholars to 'borrow' from Greek (and from Latin, which itself 'borrowed' from Greek) when they wanted to make up new words. This means that, just by reflecting on the language we use, we can get a head start in understanding the language of the New Testament.

Take a look at the words in Table 1.1. They are all derived from Greek, and each one consists of two parts joined together. For every word, separate the two parts and have a guess at the meaning of each part. Words that use the same elements are found together, so if you can't guess the meaning by looking at one word, try going on to the next one. You may find an English dictionary helpful for this.

Just knowing the information in this table means you can form about 100 Greek words! For example, what word would mean 'fear of books'? What about 'the study of writing/drawing'?

THE GREEK ALPHABET

In Greek, of course, these words would *look* rather different: Greek uses a different alphabet. This is what most often puts people off learning the language: the strange-looking characters make it seem very difficult to get to grips with. Once you have learned the letters, however, learning Greek will feel much more possible. If you have done maths or physics to any level you may find that you recognize some of the letters as they are often used

Table 1.1

Word	Meaning	Breaks up into	Meaning
anthropology	study of human beings	anthropo- -logy	human study
biology			
biography			
bibliography			
photography			
photophobia			
hydrophobia			
hydrotherapy			
psychotherapy			
psychology			

in formulae; for example, most people will recognize the letter π from their learning of maths. Even if you don't recognize any of the letters, do not despair. A little practice will soon make these letters much more familiar and easy to read.

At this early stage of learning Greek it is good to look at some Greek words every day. With regular practice you will soon find that the Greek alphabet becomes 'second nature' and you will be able to read and pronounce words without difficulty.

Things to Notice

- σ and ς: there are two forms of the letter sigma. When it appears at the end of a word it looks like this: ς, but anywhere else in the word it looks like this: σ.

- ζ and ξ: these two letters have sounds similar to our English 'z' and 'x' respectively, but look very strange. You might like to practise writing them by hand to remind you of how they look.

- ρ : looks like a 'p' but is an 'r' sound, worth making an effort to remember.

- θ, φ and ψ: these are made up of what in English would be two letters put together: 'th', 'ph' and 'ps' respectively. In Greek these are indicated by a single letter.

- χ: made up of 'ch' put together. It is not pronounced as in the English word 'chair', it is pronounced as in the Scottish 'loch' or the German 'Bach'.

- some vowels in Greek have a short and a long form: ε and η, ο and ω are examples of this.

- ι changes its pronunciation when it is at the beginning of the word. Normally it is pronounced 'i' as in 'hit' but when it begins a word it is pronounced 'y' instead, for example, Ἰωαννης is pronounced Yōannēs.

Write out the Greek alphabet (lowercase only). Take special note of any letters that you find difficult, and keep practising them until they feel natural to you.

Name	Upper-case letter	Lower-case letter	Transliteration	Approximate Pronunciation
Alpha	A	α	a	a (as in hat)
Beta	B	β	b	b
Gamma	Γ	γ	g	g (as in gold)
Delta	Δ	δ	d	d
Epsilon	E	ε	e	e (as in get)
Zeta	Z	ζ	z	dz (as in adze)
Eta	H	η	e	ê (as in fête)
Theta	Θ	θ	th	th (as in thin)
Iota	I	ι	i	i (as in hit or machine)
Kappa	K	κ	k, c	k (as in kite)
Lambda	Λ	λ	l	l (as in light)
Mu	M	μ	m	m
Nu	N	ν	n	n
Xi	Ξ	ξ	x	ks (as in kicks)
Omicron	O	o	o	o (as in hot)
Pi	Π	π	p	p
Rho	P	ρ	r	r
Sigma	Σ	σ, ς	s	s (as in sing)
Tau	T	τ	t	t
Upsilon	Υ	υ	u, y	u (as in put or truth)
Phi	Φ	φ	ph	ph, f (as in phone)
Chi	X	χ	ch, kh	ch (as in loch)
Psi	Ψ	ψ	ps	ps (as in cups)
Omega	Ω	ω	o	o (as in stone)

Putting it into Practice

Transliterate the Greek words below. That is, change the Greek letters into English letters using the table above. In each case, can you think of an English word that is similar to the Greek one? If you're not clear, try *saying* the word:[1]

γυμνασια	εμπορια
δογμα	καταστροφη
εγω	κοσμος
εθος	

COMBINATIONS OF LETTERS

Diphthongs

Like English, Greek has diphthongs (two vowels put together to make a new sound). These are:

αι	'ai' as in aisle
ει	'ei' as in weight
οι	'oi' as in foil
αυ	'ow' as in cow
ευ	'eu' as in ewe
ου	'oo' as in food
υι	'uee' as in queen

Any other vowels that appear together are not pronounced differently. Instead each vowel sound is pronounced in turn. For example, ια is pronounced 'i-a' and εα as 'e-a'.

Iota Subscript

Another feature is where an 'ι' occurs underneath α, η or ω. This is known as the iota subscript (because it occurs under the script). It does not change the pronunciation of the vowel at all (in other words you just ignore it). It looks like this:

ᾳ   ῃ   ῳ

Consonants

Some consonants also change pronunciation slightly when placed together. This occurs when γ is used alongside other letters, particularly another γ, κ, χ and ξ. When it does you pronounce it nasally (i.e. through the nose); this is most easily described in English as adding an 'n'. Examples of this that have come into English are σπογγος or 'sponge' and φαλαγξ or 'phalanx'.

Here are some Greek words (with translations) that are also found in English. In English, their pronunciation and meaning may both be slightly different. Try pronouncing each word, and identifying an English word related to it:[2]

ουρανος (sky)	οικονομια (household management)
αγγελος (messenger)	ευχαριστια (gratitude)
εικων (image)	αιων (age)
ειδωλον (image)	αυτοματος (by itself)
λαρυγξ (throat)	χαρισμα (gifted)

Did you Know?

Chi-rho (χ, ρ) often depicted like this

is a monogram thought to represent the first two Greek letters of the name Christ (χριστος).

The fish became used as a symbol within early Christianity because the Greek for 'fish' (ἰχθυς) forms an acrostic (a word made up of the first letter of a list of other words) of the first letters of the words 'Jesus Christ, Son of God Saviour':

'Ιησους – Jesus

Χριστος – Christ

Θεου – of God

'Υιος – Son

Σωτηρ – Saviour

HARD AND SOFT BREATHINGS AND ACCENTS

Some words in Greek have markings above them (e.g. ἄνθρω-πος). Some of these are breathings and others are accents.

Hard and Soft Breathings

Every word in Greek that begins with a vowel has a breathing mark: either a soft one (ἐ – pronounced 'e') or a hard one (ἑ – pronounced 'he'). The soft breathing makes no difference to the pronunciation of the vowel but the rough breathing does. You may have noticed from the table that the Greek alphabet has no 'h' sound. This is because the 'h' sound is marked at the beginning of words by the rough breathing mark. In the middle of words the sound is incorporated into a letter (e.g. θ or φ).

Note: you cannot have a breathing in the middle of a word nor can you have a breathing over a consonant.

The only exception to this is ρ, which acts a little like a vowel and whenever it begins a word it has a rough breathing above it, as in ῥητορ or ῥυθμος. In English these words are written with a 'rh' at the beginning (rhetoric, rhythm) but the hard breathing makes little real difference to the pronunciation.

When a breathing occurs at the beginning of a word that begins with a single vowel, the breathing appears directly above that vowel (e.g. ἁγιογραφια) but when the word begins with a diphthong the breathing appears over the second vowel. You will encounter some examples of this later in the chapter.

Accents

Accents exist in Greek to help you to know where the stress lies in the word. There are different kinds of accents but by the time of New Testament Greek they were all pronounced the same. Their only use for us now is to help us pronounce the words with the emphasis in the right place.

For example:

acute	circumflex	grave
λόγος	ἀρχῇ	θεὸς
Lo - gos	Ar - **che**	The - **os**

You will often see breathings and accents combined at the start of a word (e.g. ἵνα). Where this occurs the breathing is given first and the accent second (or in the case of the circumflex the accent will be above the breathing, for example, ἦν). Whenever this occurs in the Greek New Testament, remember that the breathing is much more important than the accent.

Throughout this course we will not, as a rule, indicate accents when talking about individual words – this makes the text much clearer when you are starting to read Greek. When we quote sentences from the Greek New Testament, however, the accents will be included and you might like to practise looking at them so that you become familiar with what accented words look like.

These words give practice in recognizing hard and soft breathing. Again, make a point of *speaking* these words out loud, so that you can hear how the breathing affects the sound. You may recognize English words that are based on them:[3]

ἀδης

Εὐφρατης

Ἑλλενικος

Ἑβραιος

Ἱέριχω

ἰδιωτης

ὡσαννα

STEMS AND ENDINGS

Quite often a Greek word looks very much like its English equivalent, except that the ending is different. These endings are important in Greek, but at this stage they can be a distraction. For the moment it is better to concentrate on the main body of the word (the stem) where you are more likely to find something you recognize.

Do you recognize the following words? If not, try dropping the last one, two or three letters. Do you recognize them now?[4]

βαπτισμα
ἐνεργεια
φιλοσοφια

προφητης
ὑποκριτης

βιβλος
διαλεκτος

μαρτυρος (remember: υ can be written 'y')
ὀρφανος
παραλυτικος

Often it helps if you say the word out loud to yourself.

Say each of these examples out loud. For each of the examples below, think of an English word that *sounds* similar.[5]

ἀγνοστος	ἱστορεω	ἱλαρος
καμηλος	φαντασια	ψαλμος

WRITING GREEK IN NEW TESTAMENT TIMES

The Greek that you get in a modern Greek New Testament looks quite a lot like a modern English translation. The books are broken down into chapters and verses. The Greek itself is arranged in sentences, which begin with capital letters. The words are separated by spaces, and there are punctuation and accents to help us understand the text. We can see all these features, for example, in John 1.1. Try reading this passage out loud:

Ἐν ἀρχη ἦν ὁ λογος, και ὁ λογος ἦν προς τον θεον, και θεος ἦν ὁ λογος.

All of these features are later introductions. When the New Testament books were first written, they were written in capitals; the words were not separated, but formed a continuous line of letters; accents had not yet been invented. And as already mentioned, there was no punctuation. The original text of John 1.1 would have looked more like this:

ΕΝΑΡΧΗΗΝΟΛΟΓΟΣΚΑΙΟΛΟΓΟΣΗΝΠΡΟΣΤΟΝΘΕΟ
ΝΚΑΙΘΕΟΣΗΝΟΛΟΓΟΣ

This meant that early readers of the New Testament had to work out for themselves where one word ended and another began, and where a sentence should stop. Most of the time it is quite clear from the overall context how a passage is to be understood. However, there are a few places where the way a passage is broken down and punctuated can really alter the meaning. For example, there are several different ways of understanding this passage:

ὧν   οἱ πατερες και ἐξ   ὧν   ὁ Χριστος το

Of-them the patriarchs and from them the Christ   (the)

κατα   σαρκα, ὁ   ὧν ἐπι παντων θεος εὐλογητος

according-to flesh, the-one being over   all   God   praised

εἰς τους αἰῳνας, αμην.
unto the ages, Amen

(Romans 9.5)

The NRSV translates the passage like this:

> To them belong the patriarchs, and from them, according to the flesh, comes the Messiah, who is over all, God blessed for ever. Amen.

This fits the orthodox Christian understanding of Christ: on this reading, Paul is calling Christ God.

But different readings can be found if the punctuation is changed. For example, if there were a full stop after 'all', the passage would read like this:

> To them belong the patriarchs, and from them, according to the flesh, comes the Messiah, who is over all. God be blessed for ever. Amen.

This suggests that Christ has been placed over all things by the Father, but is not himself God. It is a point of view that is now considered heretical but was clearly held by many early Christians. Was Paul one of them?

Alternatively, if there were a full stop after 'Messiah', the passage would read like this:

> To them belong the patriarchs, and from them, according to the flesh, comes the Messiah. May God, who is over all, be blessed for ever. Amen.

On this reading, Christ is not being given divine power at all. Jesus may just be a holy man.

Which of these is the right reading? Translators will choose according to what they expect to be the case.

EXPLORING GREEK FURTHER ON THE INTERNET OR WITH A DICTIONARY

For some of the work in this book you will need access either to the Internet or to some basic books on New Testament Greek. We recommend the use of the Internet as an aid to your Greek study because a number of powerful tools are available on it free of charge. However, for those who are not comfortable with this way of working, the exercises are structured so that they can be completed with the help of a basic Greek–English dictionary and an interlinear Greek–English New Testament.

If you are using the Internet, go to the website http://bible.crosswalk.com/Lexicons/NewTestamentGreek. (This is part of the very versatile *Crosswalk* site, which you may want to explore more thoroughly. If so, go to their home page for a more complete list of what they offer.) You should now be looking at something like this:

The New Testament Greek Lexicon

Enter a Strong's Number, Greek or English Word, select a translation and type from the drop-down boxes and click "Find"

(Maximum Entry for Strong's Number is 5674)

King James Version Lexicon

English Word

Click to browse the KJV or NAS Greek Lexicon

Find Help

Click on the arrow to the right of the box that says 'English Word', and select 'Greek Word' instead. (You may want to download the BST font so that you can view the Greek. If so, follow the instructions on the page.)

You can now type a Greek word into the empty box (using English letters, as on the first page of this chapter) and click on 'Find', and it will give you the dictionary definition. For example, if you want to find the meaning of the word πνευμα, type in 'pneuma' and it will give you a choice of three possible words. Click on the right one and you will find the following:

Definition

1. the third person of the triune God, the Holy Spirit, coequal, coeternal with the Father and the Son
    a. sometimes referred to in a way which emphasises his personality and character (the \\Holy\\ Spirit)
    b. sometimes referred to in a way which emphasises his work and power (the Spirit of \\Truth\\)
    c. never referred to as a depersonalised force
2. the spirit, i.e. the vital principal by which the body is animated
    a. the rational spirit, the power by which the human being feels, thinks, decides
    b. the soul
3. a spirit, i.e. a simple essence, devoid of all or at least all grosser matter, and possessed of the power of knowing, desiring, deciding, and acting
    a. a life giving spirit
    b. a human soul that has left the body
    c. a spirit higher than man but lower than God, i.e. an angel
        1. used of demons, or evil spirits, who were conceived as inhabiting the bodies of men
        2. the spiritual nature of Christ, higher than the highest angels and equal to God, the divine nature of Christ
4. the disposition or influence which fills and governs the soul of any one

a. the efficient source of any power, affection, emotion, desire, etc.
5. a movement of air (a gentle blast)
   a. of the wind, hence the wind itself
   b. breath of nostrils or mouth

If you are using a printed lexicon, you can instead go direct to the word πνευμα. Words are arranged in alphabetical order, just as in an English dictionary.

Which of these meanings lies behind the English word 'pneumatic'?

On the website or using a dictionary, find out the meaning of the following words:

ἐγω   εἰμι   ὁδος   και   ἀληθεια   ζωη

Write down two or three different meanings for each word.

Using this knowledge translate the following phrase from John 14.6:

ἐγω εἰμι ἡ ὁδος και ἡ ἀληθεια και ἡ ζωη. (translate ἡ as 'the')

See how many different translations you can make!

Note: using this website or a Greek–English dictionary will only give you the 'dictionary form' of a word. As you will discover, Greek words change according to the role they have in a sentence. One of the key skills you will be learning in future weeks is how to work out the 'dictionary form' of a word so that you can look it up.

REVIEW OF LEARNING

In this chapter we have looked at:

- the Greek alphabet and the basic shapes of the letters;

- issues affecting the pronunciation of Greek words;

- the markings that appear above the words;

- the difference that spaces and punctuation make.

Notes

1 Gymnasium, dogma, ego, ethos, emporium, catastrophe, cosmos.
2 Uranus (originally one of the gods and now one of the planets), angel, icon (a religious picture), idol, larynx, economy, eucharist (Holy Communion), aeon, automatic, charisma.
3 Hades, Euphrates, Hellenic, Hebrew, Jericho, idiot and hosanna.
4 Baptism, energy, philosophy, prophet, hypocrite, Bible (the general word for 'book' in Greek), dialect, martyr, orphan, paralytic.
5 Agnostic, history, hilarious, camel, fantasy, psalm.

2

Finding Your Way Around a Sentence

This chapter introduces you to translating for yourself. A lot of translation is based on what we might call 'informed guesswork': the reader knows some of the words, and can make a good guess about how they all fit together. For most of the time this 'informed guesswork' is good enough. It gives you a sense of how the passage is put together, its sound and rhythm, and can lead to a significantly deeper understanding of the Scriptures. There are some tasks (for example, translating the Bible into a new language) for which it is necessary to be very precise and careful about your translation; but since we are blessed with excellent English translations, Greek dictionaries and biblical commentaries, few of us are ever likely to need that very specialized knowledge.

In this chapter we will look at three ways of improving your guesswork: knowing the 'little words', using what we know about punctuation and spotting words that are the same in Greek and English. As we go, there will be sentences to practise on, bringing together all these forms of 'guessing'. You may be surprised at how much you can do already!

USEFUL LITTLE WORDS

When you are confronted with a block of Greek text, filled with words that you don't know, it can seem rather daunting! Another source of confusion is the fact that most Greek words change their endings depending on the role they are taking in the sentence. This means that students can easily get confused and discouraged: a lot of the words in front of them seem unfamiliar, and the sentences are long and complex. The purpose of this section is to introduce you to words that will help you find your way. They are short and easily recognizable. Most important, they never change their form. In other words, what you see here is exactly what you will find in a Greek sentence.

'Signpost' Words

Like English, Greek builds complex thoughts and ideas out of smaller, simpler units. **Letters** are linked together to form **words**; a few **words** link together to form a single phrase or **clause**; several clauses, each containing a single idea, are then put together to form a complex **sentence**. When students are learning to translate, they sometimes try to make the jump straight from understanding individual words to understanding whole sentences. This is making life far too difficult – a sentence may contain more than a hundred words, and by the time you've reached the end of it you will have forgotten what happened at the beginning! Instead, learn to read a sentence as a string of individual clauses: each of these is small enough to understand on its own. In the following example in English, each clause has its own square brackets:

[**If**, **therefore**, the whole church comes together] [**and** all speak in tongues,] [**and** outsiders and unbelievers enter,] [(**then**) will they not say that you are out of your mind?]

(1 Corinthians 14.23)

You can see four clauses here, each of which makes sense on its own. They are joined together by some 'signpost' words, **conjunctions**. They tell you when you are moving from one clause to the next. If you learn to recognize these conjunctions in Greek, you will be able to break the text down into 'bite-size pieces'. Try identifying the clauses in the two examples following; each has three clauses. Make a list of the 'little words' that join them together:

> the Spirit helps us in our weakness; for we do not know how to pray as we ought, but that very Spirit intercedes with sighs too deep for words.
>
> (Romans 8.26)

> he appeared to the eleven themselves as they were sitting at the table; and he upbraided them for their lack of faith and stubbornness, because they had not believed those who saw him after he had risen.
>
> (Mark 16.14)

Your list should include the following words: and, because, but, for. In English, they always occur as the first word in the clause.

Very similar words are used in Greek. The most common of these is καὶ, usually translated 'and'. Other very common ones are:

ἀλλα	but
εἰ	if, whether
ἐαν	if, whether
ἱνα	in order that
ὁτι	that, because, for

The following are also very common. But *take care*! These are never the first word in the clause (which is how they appear in English); they are usually the *second* word. So, for example, the English phrase 'I waited for the bus, **but it** never arrived' would translate in Greek as 'I waited for the bus, **it but** never arrived'.

δε	often translated 'and', but only in a weak sense: its main job is not to *mean* anything, but just to link clauses. It may sometimes be translated 'but'

γαρ   for, since

οὖν   therefore

ὅταν, ὅτε   when, whenever, while

Sometimes these words are linked together to add extra meaning:

και . . . και . . .   both . . . and

δε και   but also

μεν . . . δε . . .   on the one hand . . . on the other hand

Try out your skills with conjunctions on these sentences. Put each clause in brackets in both the English translation and the Greek. Then underline the conjunctions in Greek (remember to use the lists of useful little words above to help you):[1]

1 Matthew 10.17

[But] beware of them, for they will hand you over to councils and flog you in their synagogues;

Προσέχετε δὲ ἀπὸ τῶν ἀνθρώπων· παραδώσουσιν γὰρ ὑμᾶς εἰς συνέδρια καὶ ἐν ταῖς συναγωγαῖς αὐτῶν μαστιγώσουσιν ὑμᾶς·

2 1 Corinthians 16.10

[And] if Timothy comes, see that he has nothing to fear among you, for he is doing the work of the Lord just as I am;

Ἐὰν δὲ ἔλθῃ Τιμόθεος, βλέπετε, ἵνα ἀφόβως γένηται πρὸς ὑμᾶς· τὸ γὰρ ἔργον κυρίου ἐργάζεται ὡς καγώ·

3 1 Corinthians 16.6

and perhaps I will stay with you or even spend the winter, so that you may send me on my way, wherever I go.

πρὸς ὑμᾶς δὲ τυχὸν παραμενῶ ἢ καὶ παραχειμάσω, ἵνα ὑμεῖς με προπέμψητε οὗ ἐὰν πορεύωμαι.

Negatives

These are also very useful. They are very common, easy to identify, and have a very important role in a sentence! For example,
'God hates sinners' is different to 'God does **not** hate sinners'!
You know that wherever they crop up, you are in a clause where
something is *not* happening. In Greek, the most common words
for 'not' are:

- οὐ, οὐκ, οὐχ: these are three forms of the same word. If the
  next word begins with a consonant (except ρ) it takes the first
  form (οὐ); if it begins with a vowel with smooth breathing it
  takes the second form (οὐκ); if it begins with a ρ or a vowel
  with rough breathing it takes the third form (οὐχ). This is
  simply because it is easier to say, for example, οὐκ οἶδα than οὐ
  οἶδα.

- μη: this is much more straightforward, and always has the
  same form.

With this knowledge, you should now be able to 'navigate'
round a more complex Greek text. Break up the following Greek
passages into clauses by putting brackets round them, using your
knowledge of conjunctions. Then underline the Greek clauses
that contain negatives:[2]

1 Matthew 9.13

   [But] go and learn what this means, 'I desire mercy, not sacrifice.'
   For I have come to call not the righteous but sinners.

   πορευθέντες δὲ μάθετε τί ἐστιν· ἔλεος θέλω καὶ οὐ θυσίαν·
   οὐ γὰρ ἦλθον καλέσαι δικαίους ἀλλὰ ἁμαρτωλούς.

2 Luke 8.52

   They were all weeping and wailing for her; but he said, 'Do not
   weep; for she is not dead but sleeping.'

   ἔκλαιον δὲ πάντες καὶ ἐκόπτοντο αὐτήν. ὁ δὲ εἶπεν· μὴ
   κλαίετε, οὐ γὰρ ἀπέθανεν ἀλλὰ καθεύδει.

3 Luke 21.9

[And] when you hear of wars and insurrections, do not be terrified; for these things must take place first, but the end will not follow immediately.

ὅταν δὲ ἀκούσητε πολέμους καὶ ἀκαταστασίας, μὴ πτο-
ηθῆτε· δεῖ γὰρ ταῦτα γενέσθαι πρῶτον, ἀλλ' οὐκ εὐθέως τὸ τέλος.

4 1 Corinthians 16.11

Therefore let no one despise him. [But] send him on his way in peace, so that he may come to me; for I am expecting him with the brothers.

μή τις οὖν αὐτὸν ἐξουθενήσῃ. προπέμψατε δὲ αὐτὸν ἐν εἰρήνῃ, ἵνα ἔλθῃ πρός με· ἐκδέχομαι γὰρ αὐτὸν μετὰ τῶν ἀδελφῶν.

Prepositions

Prepositions are called this because they are 'positioned before' the word they are referring to. They can also be seen as being *about* 'position': they tell you how the noun (person, place or thing) they are referring to is related to others. Here are some of the commonest prepositions:

ἀπο	(away) from
εἰς	into
ἐκ (or ἐξ)	out of
ἐν	in, on
ἐπι	on
ἐξω	outside of
περι	about
προ	before
προς	towards
ἀνα	up

These are all quite simple. They usually come directly before the noun they are referring to, and always have more or less the same translation.

There are some other common prepositions that have *more than one* meaning:

δια	on account of/through
κατα	according to/against
μετα	after/with
παρα	to beside/from beside/at the side of
ὑπερ	above/on behalf of
ὑπο	under/by

Clearly it's possible to get quite confused here. For example, what is the difference between saying, 'I'll go to the shops **with** (μετα) you' and 'I'll go to the shops **after** (μετα) you'? The way Greek solves this is to change the ending of the noun that is being referred to. For example, look at the difference between the following:

1 John 17.20

I ask not only on behalf of these, but also on behalf of those who will believe in me **through** their **word**,

Οὐ περὶ τούτων δὲ ἐρωτῶ μόνον, ἀλλὰ καὶ περὶ τῶν πιστευόντων **διὰ** τοῦ **λόγου** αὐτῶν εἰς ἐμέ,

2 Matthew 13.21

yet such a person has no root, but endures only for a while, and when trouble or persecution arises **on account of** the **word**, that person immediately falls away.

οὐκ ἔχει δὲ ῥίζαν ἐν ἑαυτῷ ἀλλὰ πρόσκαιρος ἐστιν, γενομένης δὲ θλίψεως ἢ διωγμοῦ **διὰ** τὸν **λόγον** εὐθὺς σκανδαλίζεται.

This difference in the noun ending signifies that the noun has a different role in the sentence. We will cover this in more detail in a later chapter.

Practice at using the 'Useful Little Words'

Here are some sentences that use prepositions. They all refer to Jerusalem. The prepositions have been left out of the English translations. Put in an appropriate one in each case. Check your answers against an English New Testament:

1 Luke 10.30

Jesus replied, 'A man was going down . . . Jerusalem to Jericho, and fell into the hands of robbers, who stripped him, beat him, and went away, leaving him half dead'.

Ὑπολαβὼν ὁ Ἰησοῦς εἶπεν· ἄνθρωπος τις κατέβαινεν **ἀπὸ Ἰερουσαλὴμ** εἰς Ἰεριχὼ καὶ λῃσταῖς περιέπεσεν, οἳ καὶ ἐκδύσαντες αὐτὸν καὶ πληγὰς ἐπιθέντες ἀπῆλθον ἀφέντες ἡμιθανῆ.

2 Luke 18.31

Then he took the twelve aside and said to them, 'See, we are going up . . . Jerusalem, and everything that is written about the Son of Man by the prophets will be accomplished'.

Παραλαβὼν δὲ τοὺς δώδεκα εἶπεν πρὸς αὐτούς· ἰδοὺ ἀναβαίνομεν **εἰς Ἰερουσαλήμ**, καὶ τελεσθήσεται πάντα τὰ γεγραμμένα διὰ τῶν προφητῶν τῷ υἱῷ τοῦ ἀνθρώπου·

3 Acts 9.13

But Ananias answered, 'Lord, I have heard from many about this man, how much evil he has done to your saints . . . Jerusalem'

ἀπεκρίθη δὲ Ἀνανίας· κύριε, ἤκουσα ἀπὸ πολλῶν περὶ τοῦ ἀνδρὸς τούτου ὅσα κακὰ τοῖς ἁγίοις σου ἐποίησεν **ἐν Ἰερουσαλήμ**·

4 Acts 22.18

and saw Jesus saying to me, 'Hurry and get . . . Jerusalem quickly, because they will not accept your testimony about me.'

καὶ ἰδεῖν αὐτὸν λέγοντα μοι· σπεῦσον καὶ ἔξελθε ἐν τάχει **ἐξ Ἰερουσαλήμ**, διότι οὐ παραδέξονταί σου μαρτυρίαν περὶ ἐμοῦ.

Which of these prepositions express the idea of movement? Which would you use if you wanted to say, 'I live in Jerusalem'?[3]

PUNCTUATION

Compared to the system of accents, Greek punctuation is easy. The Greek New Testament has four sorts of punctuation, and two of them are just as in English:

.	full stop
,	comma
·	colon or semicolon (raised above the line)
;	question mark

Punctuation is another way of breaking up a passage into 'bite-size pieces'. If you don't know what one phrase means, it's possible to jump over it and work it out by looking at the next one. For example, if you know just one phrase in this passage you can work out several others:

1 Peter 2.9

But you are a chosen race, a **royal priesthood**, a holy nation, God's own people, in order that you may proclaim the mighty acts of him who called you out of darkness into his marvellous light.

ὑμεῖς δὲ γένος ἐκλεκτόν, **βασίλειον ἱεράτευμα**, ἔθνος ἅγιον, λαὸς εἰς περιποίησιν, ὅπως τὰς ἀρετὰς ἐξαγγείλητε τοῦ ἐκ σκότους ὑμᾶς καλέσαντος εἰς τὸ θαυμαστὸν αὐτοῦ φῶς·

The phrase for 'royal priesthood' is given in bold letters in the Greek passage. It is the second in a list of four phrases separated by commas. So by seeing where the commas come in the Greek text above, you should be able to write down the phrases for:

chosen race (literally a select family)

holy nation

God's own people (literally a people for possession)

Note the number of different words that are used here to describe people: γενος, ἐθνος, λαος. Each word gives rise to a different English word: genealogy, ethnic and laity. Does this give you an insight into the different shades of meaning you have here? Why is it so interesting that the author has chosen to use these three words in succession here?

This trick needs to be used with caution, because sometimes the punctuation and word order are not the same in the Greek as in the English. Nevertheless, it all helps when making an informed guess.

Here is a passage where the word order is different in Greek and English, but the punctuation helps to sort out what is going on. Try reading it in English. Then write a colon (:) in the English text wherever you see a · in the Greek, and a question mark (?) in the English wherever you see a ; in the Greek. Add in the capital letters beginning sentences and after each colon, and the full stops. Does it make better sense now? Rewrite the passage in clear English and check against an English Bible:

καὶ ἠρωτησαν αὐτον· τι   οὐν; συ Ἡλιας εἰ; και λεγει· οὐκ

And they-asked   him   what then you Elijah are and he-says not

εἰμι. ὁ προφητης εἰ συ; και   ἀπεκριθη· οὐ. εἰπαν

I-am the prophet are you and he-answered no they-said

οὐν αὐτῳ· τις   εἰ;   ἱνα ἀποκρισιν δωμεν

therefore to-him who are-you so-that an-answer we-may-give

τοις   πεμψασιν ἡμας· τι   λεγεις περι σεαυτου;

to-those who-sent   us   what do-you-say about yourself

(John 1. 21–22)

Another reason to be cautious is that, as you may remember from the last chapter, the earliest Greek manuscripts had no punctuation at all. They did not even separate the words from one another. Because the punctuation was added in later, we need to be alert to the way it may have changed the original meaning. For example, here is a passage that relies heavily on the use of (inserted) question marks:

Οὐκ εἰμι ἐλευθερος; οὐκ εἰμι ἀποστολος; οὐχι Ἰησουν τον

Not I-am a-free-person not I-am an-apostle   not   Jesus [the]

κυριον ἡμων ἑορακα;   οὐ το ἐργον μου ὑμεις ἐστε ἐν κυριῳ;

Lord   our I-have-seen not [the] work my   you   are in the-Lord

(1 Corinthians 9.1)

Without the question marks, it could be translated something like this:

I am not a free person; I am not an apostle; I have not seen Jesus our Lord; you are not my work in the Lord.

Rewrite this passage in English, taking account of the question marks in the text. Check your answer against an English Bible.

In this case, we can be fairly sure that the punctuation was inserted in the right place: Paul would never deny that he was an apostle! However, as we saw in the last chapter, in a *few* places in the Bible, the way punctuation is used may be a matter for debate.

SPOTTING WORDS YOU MAY KNOW

It became clear in the last lesson that we already know a lot of Greek. That's because many words (particularly names and technical terms) are very similar in English. If you recognize just a few words in a Greek sentence, it can help you 'navigate' – to find your way around the words you don't know.

To give you practice at this basic skill, here is an exercise in guesswork. Knowing what you do about the words above, and adding in words that you can probably recognize (e.g. 'Amen') answer the questions on these passages. Recognizable words are given in **bold**. Hint: you may find it helpful to read the Greek passage out loud.[4]

1   Luke 9.19

They answered, '**John** the **Baptist**; but others, **Elijah**; and still others, that one of the ancient **prophets** has arisen.'

οἱ δὲ ἀποκριθέντες εἶπαν· Ἰωάννην τὸν βαπτιστήν, ἄλλοι δὲ Ἠλίαν, ἄλλοι δὲ ὅτι προφήτης τις τῶν ἀρχαίων ἀνέστη.

(a) Which word translates here as 'others'? (**clue:** it occurs twice)
(b) Which word means 'ancient'? (**hint:** archaic)

2 Hebrews 7.2

and to him **Abraham** apportioned 'one-tenth of everything'.
His name, in the first place, means 'king of righteousness'; next
he is also king of **Salem**, that is, 'king of peace'.

ᾧ καὶ δεκάτην ἀπὸ πάντων ἐμέρισεν Ἀβραάμ, πρῶτον μὲν
ἑρμηνευόμενος βασιλεὺς δικαιοσύνης ἔπειτα δὲ καὶ
βασιλεὺς Σαλήμ, ὅ ἐστιν βασιλεὺς εἰρήνης,

(a) What do you think is the word for 'king'? (**clue**: it crops up
three times)
(b) What are likely to be the words for 'righteousness' and
'peace'?

3 Galatians 4.25

Now **Hagar** is Mount **Sinai** in **Arabia** and corresponds to the
present **Jerusalem,** for she is in slavery with her children.

τὸ δὲ Ἀγὰρ Σινᾶ ὄρος ἐστὶν ἐν τῇ Ἀραβίᾳ· συστοιχεῖ δὲ τῇ
νῦν Ἰερουσαλήμ, δουλεύει γὰρ μετὰ τῶν τέκνων αὐτῆς.

(a) Which are likely to be the words for 'Mount', 'in', and
'present'? Check your answers with a dictionary or with
the *Crosswalk* website mentioned in Chapter 1, and write
them down.

4 Acts 6.11

Then they secretly instigated some men to say [that], 'We have
heard him speak **blasphemous** words against **Moses** and God'.

τότε ὑπέβαλον ἄνδρας λέγοντας ὅτι ἀκηκόαμεν αὐτοῦ
λαλοῦντος ῥήματα βλάσφημα εἰς Μωϋσῆν καὶ τὸν θεόν.

(a) Underline the phrase for 'Moses and God'.
(b) What is likely to be the word for 'blasphemous'?

USING TOOLS TO HELP YOU FIND YOUR WAY AROUND A SENTENCE

The following questions are designed to be answered by using web-based resources. However, they can all be completed equally easily by consulting an interlinear Greek–English New Testament and a Greek–English dictionary.

Go to the website www.ntgateway.com and click on the button for **Greek New Testament Gateway**. A web Gateway is a site that does not usually carry much material of its own; instead, it provides links to other sites in its subject area. The Greek NT Gateway puts you in touch with a wide range of useful resources. We will be using only one in this chapter, but you are encouraged to explore the others at your leisure.

The one we will use for this chapter is *The Online Greek Bible*. Get to it by clicking on the heading *The Online Greek Bible* on the Gateway web page, or by typing in www. greekbible.com. The top of the page gives you a range of options:

- Leave the Font as it is (in 'Symbol').
- Click on the arrow to the right of the box marked 'Passage' and select 'Luke' from the drop-down list. In the next 2 boxes type '1' and '5', then click 'go'. You should now be looking at the Greek text for Luke 1.5. Note that *The Online Greek Bible* does not include accents or breathing marks.

It is possible to find out more about any word written in the text by clicking on it: a window should open up which gives its meaning. If the meaning is not given, it is *usually* because the word can be transliterated directly into English (e.g. Βηθλεεμ = Bethlehem). However, there are some words for which an English translation is not given.[5]

1 Copy out Luke 1.5 and underline the Greek words for **Herod** and **Elisabeth**. You will have to work these out for yourself, because the translation will not be given on screen, but you may find it easier if you look up the verse in an English Bible.

2 Select and write out John 1.1–5. Which do you think is the Greek term for **Word**? Did you guess right? Practise reading this passage out loud until you are fluent.

3 Select Matthew 2.16. Translate the following phrases:

υπο των μαγων

εν Βηθλεεμ και εν πασι τοις οριοις

κατα τον κρονον

Note: the words τον, των and τοις can all be translated 'the'.

Write down your answers, then check them against an English translation. Do you agree with what the translators have put?

REVIEW OF LEARNING

In this chapter we have looked at ways to find your way around a sentence:

• 'useful little words' – conjunctions, negatives and prepositions;

• using punctuation;

• how to spot words you already know.

Notes

1 Your Greek passages should look like this:

(1) Matthew 10.17 [Προσέχετε δὲ ἀπὸ τῶν ἀνθρώπων·] [παραδώσουσιν γὰρ ὑμᾶς εἰς συνέδρια] [καὶ ἐν ταῖς συναγωγαῖς αὐτῶν μαστιγώσουσιν ὑμᾶς·]

(2) 1 Corinthians 16.10 [Ἐὰν δὲ ἔλθῃ Τιμόθεος,] [βλέπετε, ἵνα ἀφόβως γένηται πρὸς ὑμᾶς·] [τὸ γὰρ ἔργον κυρίου ἐργάζεται ὡς καγώ·]

(3) 1 Corinthians 16.6 [πρὸς ὑμᾶς δὲ τυχὸν παραμενῶ] [ἢ καὶ παραχειμάσω,] [ἵνα ὑμεῖς με προπέμψητε οὗ ἐὰν πορεύωμαι.]

2 Your Greek passages should look like this:

(1) Matthew 9.13 [πορευθέντες δὲ μάθετε τί ἐστιν·] [<u>ἔλεος θέλω καὶ</u> <u>οὐ θυσίαν·</u>] [<u>οὐ γὰρ ἦλθον καλέσαι δικαίους ἀλλὰ ἁμαρτωλούς.</u>]

(2) Luke 8.52 [ἔκλαιον δὲ πάντες καὶ ἐκόπτοντο αὐτήν.] [ὁ δὲ εἶπεν·] [<u>μὴ κλαίετε,</u>][<u>οὐ γὰρ ἀπέθανεν ἀλλὰ καθεύδει.</u>]

(3) Luke 21.9 [ὅταν δὲ ἀκούσητε πολέμους καὶ ἀκαταστασίας,] [<u>μὴ</u> <u>πτοηθῆτε·</u>] [δεῖ γὰρ ταῦτα γενέσθαι πρῶτον,] [ἀλλ' οὐκ εὐθέως τὸ τέλος.]

(4) 1 Corinthians 16.11 [<u>μή τις οὖν αὐτὸν ἐξουθενήσῃ.</u>] [προπέμψατε δὲ αὐτὸν ἐν εἰρήνῃ,] [ἵνα ἔλθῃ πρός με·] [ἐκδέχομαι γὰρ αὐτὸν μετὰ τῶν ἀδελφῶν.]

3 ἀπο, εἰς and ἐξ (or ἐκ) express the idea of movement. ἐν would be the preposition used to say 'I live in Jerusalem'.

4 (1a) ἄλλοι; (1b) ἀρχαίων; (2a) βασιλεὺς; (2b) δικαιοσύνης, εἰρήνης; (3) ὄρος, ἐν, νῦν; (4a) <u>Μωϋσῆν καὶ τὸν θεόν</u>; (4b) βλάσφημα.

5 (1) ηρωδου, ελισαβετ

    (2) λογος

    (3) υπο των μαγων: by the wise men; εν Βηθλεεμ και εν πασι τοις οριοις: in Bethlehem and in all the regions; κατα τον κρονον: according to the time.

3

Understanding How Greek Words Work

One of the concerns students often have when they begin to learn a language is that they will have to memorize long lists of words. There is no easy way around this problem: even on this course (which concentrates on understanding how other people have translated the New Testament rather than starting from scratch) your understanding and enjoyment will be greater the more Greek words you know. However, if you understand something of how Greek words are made up and relate to each other, you can make a little knowledge go a long way; in effect, by knowing the meaning of one word, you may be able to make a good guess at the meaning of several others.

In this chapter we will look at two ways in which Greek words relate to each other: by sharing a stem (including the distinction between different sorts of words) and by combining smaller words (including prefixes). We will then look briefly at how words interact to form sentences.

RECOGNIZING RELATED WORDS

Spotting the Stem

One of the nice things about Greek is its economy of effort: when the ancient Greeks thought up a good word stem, they'd make a lot of related words out of it by making only tiny changes.

Take the word stem ἀρχ-. In the New Testament, it helps to form (among others) the following words:

ἄρχομαι	I begin
ἄρχω	I rule
ἄρχων	ruler
ἀρχαιος	old
ἀρχη	beginning, at first
ἀρχιερευς	chief priest

All these words are to do with being 'first': first in time (like ἀρχη, and our own word 'archaeology') or first in importance (like ἄρχων, or archbishop). Knowing that, you can probably work out what these mean as well:[1]

ἀρχισυναγωγος

ἀρχαγγελος

Of course, English has the same characteristic, and that can make translating from the Greek very easy:

ἐξῆλθεν   ὁ σπείρων τοῦ σπεῖραι τὸν σπόρον αὐτοῦ.

Went-out the sower   to   sow   the   seed of-him

(Luke 8.5)

The words for 'sower', 'sow' and 'seed' are obviously related in English and also in Greek. In both cases, they *start* in the same way, but have different *endings*.

We can explore further how Greek words are made up by looking at stems such as δυνα- and βασιλ-. A selection of words derived from each word stem are given below:

δυναμαι	I am able to
δυναμις	power
δυναμω	I strengthen
δυναστης	ruler
δυνατος	strong
βασιλεια	kingdom

βασιλειον	palace
βασιλευς	king
βασιλικος	royal, kingly
βασιλευω	I rule
βασιλισσα	queen

This means that, once again, by making use of a little knowledge you can go a long way. To illustrate this, here are some sentences that include words you have already learned. The words you should recognize are in **bold** type in the English translation. Underline the equivalent words in the Greek, and answer the question for each sentence (**hint**: the *endings* in Greek might be different. Look at the *stem*.):[2]

1 Mark 13.8

For nation will rise against nation, and **kingdom** against **kingdom**; there will be earthquakes in various places; there will be famines. This is but the **beginning** of the birth pangs.

ἐγερθήσεται γὰρ ἔθνος ἐπ' ἔθνος καὶ βασιλεία ἐπὶ βασιλείαν, ἔσονται σεισμοὶ κατὰ τόπους, ἔσονται λιμοί· ἀρχὴ ὠδίνων ταῦτα.

What is the word for 'nation'? (**clue**: it occurs twice)

2 1 Corinthians 15.24

Then comes the end, when he hands over the **kingdom** to God the Father, after he has destroyed every **ruler** and every authority and **power**.

εἶτα τὸ τέλος, ὅταν παραδιδῷ τὴν βασιλείαν τῷ θεῷ καὶ πατρί, ὅταν καταργήσῃ πᾶσαν ἀρχὴν καὶ πᾶσαν ἐξουσίαν καὶ δύναμιν.

Compare the word for 'ruler' here with the word for 'beginning' in the previous example. What underlying idea links the two words?

Different Sorts of Word

In each of the cases above, the stem is used to produce not just different words, but different *sorts of* words. Some of them are the names of persons, places or things (nouns); some are used to *describe* a person, place or thing (adjectives); and some are used to say what a person, place or thing *does* (verbs). Because different types of words do different things in a sentence, it's important to be clear about this distinction. For example, if we look at a noun (like βασιλεια) and think it is a verb (like βασιλευω), we will probably misunderstand what a sentence is saying.

Mark each of the words in the lists above that have been derived from the stems ἀρχ-, βασιλ- and δυνα- as a noun (n), adjective (adj) or verb (vb). For example:[3]

ἀρχαιος	old (adj)
βασιλευω	I rule (vb)
δυναμις	power (n)

If you look any of these words up in a Greek–English dictionary, it may or may not tell you if it is a noun, adjective or verb. However, if you can't tell clearly from the meaning, you can tell from the way the word is written in Greek. Verbs are usually written simply in the form for 'I am doing . . .' (Technically known as the First Person Present Indicative Active, but more on that later); nouns are given with an extra ending; and adjectives are given with *two* extra endings. For example, in most dictionaries the entries for these three words will look something like this:

ἀρχαιος -α -ον	old (adj)
βασιλευω	I rule (vb)
δυναμις -εως	power (n)

If you look at the dictionary on the *Crosswalk* website already introduced, you will find the same information. Go to http:// bible.crosswalk.com/Lexicons/Greek and type in 'archaios' (don't forget to select 'Greek Word' in the drop-down list), click 'Find' and then click on the Greek word in blue. It will tell you all about the word, and under 'Parts of Speech' it will tell you that it is an **adjective**.

Look up the following words using a dictionary or website. In each case, work out whether the word is a noun, adjective or verb, and give the meaning of the word:[4]

1 εἰρηνη   εἰρηνικος   εἰρηνοποιεω

What is the meaning of the stem εἰρην-?

2 ἱερατευμα   ἱερατευω   ἱερος

What sort of a place would you expect Ἱεραπολις to be?

Further Practice with Stems

In the sentences below, underline the word in Greek that corresponds to the word in bold in the English version. Then indicate underneath whether that word is a noun, verb or adjective. You may be able to work this out from the context, or the stem, or a combination of both (**reminder:** the *ending* will not help you much here!). Then answer the question for each sentence.[5]

1 1 Corinthians 4.20

For the **kingdom** of God depends not on talk but on **power**.

οὐ γὰρ ἐν λόγῳ ἡ βασιλεία τοῦ θεοῦ ἀλλ' ἐν δυνάμει.

Identify the word for 'not' (**hint:** it's in a strange place!).

2 Hebrews 4.15

For we do not have a **high priest** who is un**able** to sympathize with our weaknesses, but we have one who in every respect has been tested as we are, yet without sin.

οὐ γὰρ ἔχομεν ἀρχιερέα μὴ δυνάμενον συμπαθῆσαι ταῖς ἀσθενείαις ἡμῶν, πεπειρασμένον δὲ κατὰ πάντα καθ’ ὁμοιότητα χωρὶς ἁμαρτίας.

Identify the word for 'sympathize' (**clue:** sounds like the English).

As we have seen, the same stem can be used to make new words by changing its *ending*. But on the whole in Greek sentences, you will not find the endings as they are given in your dictionary or on a website. They change depending upon the role the word has in a sentence, as they did in the examples above. This is important to bear in mind when you are looking up a word in a dictionary: you have to guess at its dictionary form in order to look it up. This is not as hard as it sounds, because when you look at your dictionary you will usually find only one or two possible words. So if you think the answer to the last question is συμπαθησαι and you look it up in your dictionary or on the website, you will not find it there; but if you look up words with the stem συμπαθ- you will find συμπαθεω. It is clearly the same verb, but with a different ending.

Practise looking up the following words, drawn from the examples in the previous section:

δυναμει   λογῳ   ἁμαρτιας

PREFIXES

Another way in which Greek 'recycles' the same stem to form different words is to add something at the *beginning* of a word. This is known as a prefix, and they're very common indeed in both Greek and English. Most often in Greek, the prefix is one of the prepositions that we looked at in the previous chapter.

For example, in this passage:

I will get up and go to my father, and I will say to him, 'Father, I have sinned against heaven, and before you;'

(Luke 15.18)

The Greek looks like this:

ἀναστὰς **πορεύσομαι πρὸς** τὸν πατέρα μου

I-will-rise-up,   go   to the father of-me

But it could just as easily be written:

ἀναστας **προσπορευσομαι** τῳ πατρι μου

I-will-rise-up,   go-to   the father of-me

Sometimes you even find the prefix to the verb and the preposition together. For example:

οὐ μὴ **εἰσ**έλθητε   **εἰς** τὴν βασιλείαν τῶν οὐρανῶν.

Not (ever) you-shall-enter-in into the kingdom   of-the heaven

(Matthew 5.20)

A verb like βαλλω (I throw, from the stem βαλ-) takes a wide range of prepositions, each of which slightly changes the meaning. Here is a list of some of the common ones:

ἀντιβαλλω	exchange, discuss ('throw back and forth')
ἀποβαλλω	throw off (clothes)
ἐμβαλλω	throw in (ἐμ is another form of ἐν, 'in')
καταβαλλω	knock down
προβαλλω	put forward
ὑπερβαλλω	surpass

What do you think might be the meaning of ἐκβαλλω? What about ἐπιβαλλω? Check your answers by consulting a dictionary or website.

This way of using prepositions as prefixes is most commonly used for verbs, but some nouns and adjectives can begin with prepositions in the same way. For example, ὑποκριτης (hypocrite) is derived from κριτης (judge). Look up the following words and see if you can spot the meaning of the shared stem:[6]

ἀναστασις   ἐκστασις   ὑποστασις

Further Practice with Prefixes

For each of the following, complete the missing word. Then identify and underline that word in the passage from the Greek Bible that follows (remember: the ending of the word may be different). The first example has been done for you:

1 If βαλλω = I throw, then ἐκβαλλω = I drive out. Find the word in the following passage:

Mark 11.15

Then they came to Jerusalem. And he entered the temple and began to drive out those who were selling and those who were buying in the temple, and he overturned the tables of the money changers and the seats of those who sold doves;

Καὶ ἔρχονται εἰς Ἱεροσόλυμα. Καὶ εἰσελθὼν εἰς τὸ ἱερὸν ἤρξατο ἐκβάλλειν τοὺς πωλοῦντας καὶ τοὺς ἀγοράζοντας ἐν τῷ ἱερῷ, καὶ τὰς τραπέζας τῶν κολλυβιστῶν καὶ τὰς καθέ- δρας τῶν πωλούντων τὰς περιστερὰς κατέστρεψεν,

2 If πορευομαι = I travel, then προσπορευομαι = ... Find
the word in the following passage:

Mark 10.35

James and John, the sons of Zebedee, came forward to him and
said to him, 'Teacher, we want you to do for us whatever we ask
of you.'

Καὶ προσπορεύονται αὐτῷ Ἰάκωβος καὶ Ἰωάννης οἱ υἱοὶ
Ζεβεδαίου λέγοντες αὐτῷ· διδάσκαλε, θέλομεν ἵνα ὃ ἐὰν
αἰτήσωμεν σε ποιήσῃς ἡμῖν.

3 If καταβαινω = I go down, then . . . . = I go up. Find the
word in the following passage:

Matthew 20.17

While Jesus was going up to Jerusalem, he took the twelve disciples aside by themselves, and said to them on the way,

Καὶ ἀναβαίνων ὁ Ἰησοῦς εἰς Ἱεροσόλυμα παρέλαβεν τοὺς
δώδεκα [μαθητὰς] κατ᾽ ἰδίαν καὶ ἐν τῇ ὁδῷ εἶπεν αὐτοῖς·

4 If βλεπω = I look, then . . . . = I look around. Find the word
in the following passage:

Mark 5.32

He looked all around to see who had done it.

καὶ περιεβλέπετο ἰδεῖν τὴν τοῦτο ποιήσασαν.

5 If βαπτω = I dip, then ἐμβαπτω = ... Find the word in the following passage:

Mark 14.20

He said to them, 'It is one of the twelve, one who is dipping bread into the bowl with me.'

ὁ δὲ εἶπεν αὐτοῖς· εἶς τῶν δώδεκα, ὁ ἐμβαπτόμενος μετ' ἐμοῦ εἰς τὸ τρύβλιον.

6 If φερω = I carry, then . . . . = I carry into. Find the word in the following passage:

Luke 12.11

When they bring you before the synagogues, the rulers, and the authorities, do not worry about how you are to defend yourselves or what you are to say;

Ὅταν δὲ εἰσφέρωσιν ὑμᾶς ἐπὶ τὰς συναγωγὰς καὶ τὰς ἀρχὰς καὶ τὰς ἐξουσίας, μὴ μεριμνήσητε πῶς ἢ τί ἀπολογήσησθε ἢ τί εἴπητε·

7 If γραφη = writing, then . . . . = inscription (writing-on). Find the word in the following passage:

Luke 20.24

'Show me a denarius. Whose head and whose title does it bear?' They said, 'The emperor's.'

δείξατέ μοι δηνάριον· τίνος ἔχει εἰκόνα καὶ ἐπιγραφήν; οἱ δὲ εἶπαν· Καίσαρος.

CHECKING YOUR ANSWERS USING A WEBSITE OR DICTIONARY

Now is a good moment to introduce you to a different website, *The Unbound Bible*. You can use this to find the meaning of any word in the New Testament, but it will only give you the dictionary form. For example, it will tell you the meaning of ἐκβαλλω but not ἐκβαλλειν (see question 1 on p. 47).

Go to *The Unbound Bible* site (http://unbound.biola.edu):

- Click on the link marked 'Greek & Hebrew Lexicon' in the blue column on the left.

- A window opens that allows you to search for a word in the dictionary. But note: *The Unbound Bible* uses a rather odd transliteration scheme. Its scheme is not designed to be spoken out loud: it just distinguishes between different Greek letters. For example, the Greek ψυχη (pronounced 'psyche' in English) has to be typed in as 'yuch' when using *The Unbound Bible*.

- We recommend that you print off *The Unbound Bible*'s way of typing Greek transliterations by clicking on the 'Greek Transliteration Chart' link under the box marked 'Search for a Greek Word'. Take special note of the English letters that this site uses for η, θ, ξ, χ, ψ and final ς.

- Try typing the word ἐκβαλλω in the box marked 'Search for a Greek Word', click 'Find Greek Word' and check your answer with question 1 on p. 47. Do the same for προσπορευομαι, ἐμβαπτω and ἐπιγραφη. Alternatively you can look these words up in a dictionary.

Further Work with *The Unbound Bible* or a Concordance

1 John 3.3

> Jesus answered him, 'Very truly, I tell you, no one can see the
> kingdom of God without being born from above.'
>
> ἀπεκρίθη Ἰησοῦς καὶ εἶπεν αὐτῷ· ἀμὴν ἀμὴν λέγω σοι, ἐὰν
> μή τις γεννηθῇ ἄνωθεν, οὐ δύναται ἰδεῖν τὴν βασιλείαν τοῦ
> θεοῦ.

What word is translated 'truly'? (You will recognize it when you
hear it.)

We will now explore how this word is used in the New Testament by using *The Unbound Bible* website. If you prefer, you can
do the same research using a concordance (such as *Strong's*) that
keeps a note of the Greek behind the New Testament text.
    Go to *The Unbound Bible* site (http://unbound.biola.edu):

- In the blue column to the left of the page you will see a number of white boxes. Open the drop-down list for the first of
  these (where it currently says 'New American Stand.') by clicking on the little arrow on the right of the box. Scroll down and
  select 'Greek NT NA 26/27' from the list. This is the best
  Greek version to work with.

- In the next box, 'Choose a Book', select 'Gospels' from the
  drop-down menu.

- You can search for the word ἀμην by typing 'amhn' into the
  box marked 'Word/s'. Click 'Search'. If you have followed the
  instructions, you should have 85 verses before you, in Greek.

- From the list of verses in front of you, look some up in your
  English Bible:
    (a) When the word is being used, who is speaking?
    (b) Does only one person use the word?

- The answers you found are scattered across all four Gospels.
  Now go back and type the word in *twice*. This will give you

all the verses in the Gospels where the word is used twice together.

   c) Are these verses scattered across the four Gospels, or concentrated in one of them?

• What conclusions do you draw from your research?

REVIEW OF LEARNING

In this chapter we have looked at:

• how to recognize words that are related in meaning;

• how to work out the function of a word in a sentence (noun, verb, adjective);

• the use of prefixes to alter the meaning of a word.

Notes

1 The head of a synagogue; a high-ranking angel.

2 (1) ἐθνος. (2) 'being first'.

3 ἀρχομαι (vb), ἀρχω (vb), ἀρχων (n), ἀρχαιος (adj), ἀρχη (n), ἀρχιερευς (n), ἀρχισυναγωγος (n), ἀρχαγγελος (n), δυναμαι (vb), δυναμις (n), δυναμω (vb), δυναστης (adj), δυνατος (adj), βασιλεια (n), βασιλειον (n), βασιλευς (n), βασιλικος (adj), βασιλευω (vb), βασιλισσα (n).

4 (1) εἰρηνη – peace (n); εἰρηνικος – peaceful (adj); εἰρηνοποιεω – I make peace (vb). The stem would therefore mean 'peace'. (2) ἱερατευμα – priesthood (n); ἱερατευω – function as a priest (vb); ἱερος – sacred (adj). Ἱεραπολις would therefore be a 'sacred city' or possibly a 'city of priests'.

5 (1) 1 Corinthians 4.20: οὐ γὰρ ἐν λόγῳ ἡ βασιλεία (n) τοῦ θεοῦ ἀλλ' ἐν δυνάμει (n). The word for 'not' is οὐ. (2) Hebrews 4.15 οὐ γὰρ ἔχομεν ἀρχιερέα (n) μὴ δυνάμενον (vb) συμπαθῆσαι ταῖς ἀσθενείαις ἡμῶν, πεπειρασμένον δὲ κατὰ πάντα καθ' ὁμοιότητα χωρὶς ἁμαρτίας. The word for 'sympathize' is συμπαθησαι.

6 ἀναστασις – resurrection (getting up); ἐκστασις – amazement (standing outside); ὑποστασις – conviction (standing under).

4

Introduction to Nouns and Their Endings

In the last chapter, we noted in passing that the *endings* of words often change depending on the work they do in a sentence. We saw how this affects their meaning in relation to prepositions. In this chapter we will explore **nouns**: words that name persons (e.g. John), places (e.g. Birmingham) or things (e.g. table). We will look at how their endings change depending on the work they have to do in a sentence. We will then go on to look at related words (the definite article and pronouns).

UNDERSTANDING NOUNS

The Basics: How Nouns Work

In English, the work each noun does in a sentence is usually indicated by the word order. For example, in the sentence 'Jesus gave bread to the disciples', 'Jesus' comes first because it is the main **subject**. This is followed by the verb; then comes 'bread', which is the **object** (the thing that the subject is doing something to). Last of all comes 'the disciples', which fills in the detail of the sentence. This last bit is termed the **indirect object**: those who or that which the action is 'for' or 'to'.

In Greek, the word order is much less important. The same sentence could be written like this:

ὁ Ἰησους ἐδωκεν ἀρτον τοις μαθηταις

Jesus   gave   bread to-the disciples

But it could just as easily be written in one of the following ways:

τοις μαθηταις ἐδωκεν ἀρτον ὁ ᾽Ιησους

to-the disciples gave   bread   Jesus

or:

ἀρτον ὁ ᾽Ιησους τοις μαθηταις ἐδωκεν

bread   Jesus   to-the disciples gave

or:

ὁ ᾽Ιησους ἀρτον ἐδωκεν τοις μαθηταις

Jesus   bread   gave   to-the disciples

(see Matthew 26.26)

Which raises the question: how can you tell the difference, in Greek, between 'Jesus gave bread to the disciples' and 'The disciples gave Jesus to the bread'?

The answer is all in the endings. If you look at Table 4.1 you will notice that the first three letters are the same (λογ-), but the last two or three letters are different. Greek nouns have a stem that usually remains the same, and an ending that changes depending on the work they have to do. The ending tells you how the noun fits into the sentence (the **case**) and whether it is referring to one (singular) or more (plural) individuals (the **number**).

In addition to these there is a third thing to look out for. In Greek all nouns have a **gender**: masculine, feminine or neuter. We might expect that all women are feminine, all men are masculine and all things (like tables) are neuter. While it is true that men are always in the masculine (so the name Πετρος is masculine) and women are always in the feminine (so the name Μαριας is feminine), things (like tables) are not always in the neuter. In fact many nouns are masculine or feminine even though it is not clear to us why this would be the case. So, for example, 'word' (λογος) is masculine, 'heart' (καρδια) is feminine and 'book' (βιβλιον) is neuter. In this chapter we will concentrate on masculine nouns with -ος endings. We will look at the most common forms of feminine and neuter nouns in Chapter 5.

Cases in More Detail

As in the example above, a sentence may contain a number of different nouns. We can tell which role each one takes in the sentence by its **case**, which is reflected in its **ending**. There are five cases in Greek, and we will look in some detail at four of them in this chapter. Take the sentence:

Jesus announced the Kingdom of God to the World.

The *subject* of a sentence is the person or thing that is doing the verb. In this sentence the subject is Jesus, because he is doing the announcing: Jesus announces. To work out the subject, find the verb (here 'announce') and then ask 'Who is doing the announcing?' The answer is 'Jesus'. The subject takes the **nominative** case: this is simply the grammatical name for subject.

As well as a subject, the verb may have a *direct object*. To work out whether it does, and if so what it is, turn the sentence into a question. Here we would ask 'Jesus announced what?' The answer is 'the Kingdom' so this is the direct object. The direct object takes the **accusative** case.

The *possessive*, as its name suggests, indicates that something belongs to something or someone else. We mark this in English either by using the word 'of' or by marking possession with an apostrophe ('). So, for example, in this sentence we can see that a possessive is present because of the word 'of'. 'Of God' can also be written in English as 'God's' (kingdom) and it means exactly the same thing. The possessive is in the **genitive** case.

Finally some sentences will also have an *indirect object*. An indirect object is usually the recipient of the direct object. So in this sentence Jesus announced the Kingdom of God 'to the world'. We can see that the world is the recipient of the message of the Kingdom. In grammars and commentaries you will find this called the **dative**. In Greek the dative is a little confusing because it can also be used to indicate instrument ('by means of' or 'with') or place ('in' or 'at'). What you should be aware of is that you can translate this case by adding one of the following words or phrases:

to
for
by means of
with
in
at

If in any doubt try them in turn until one makes sense!

There is also the **vocative** case. This is used when somebody is being spoken to directly, but it is quite unusual and easy to spot. It need not worry us here.

Looking at Endings

Let's begin by looking at all the endings for the word λογος. You will find all of these in the Greek New Testament, and they all mean the same thing: 'word' or 'words' (Table 4.1).

Table 4.1

	Singular	Plural
Nominative	λογος	λογοι
Accusative	λογον	λογους
Genitive	λογου	λογων
Dative	λογῳ	λογοις

From what you see in Table 4.1 can you work out what is the stem (i.e. the bit that always stays the same) and what is the ending of each word (i.e. what is left after you have taken the stem off)?

Using Your Knowledge of Endings

When you look at a word in Greek you want to discover various things:

- What the stem means (i.e. the bit of the word that never changes). To do this you need to identify the stem, and then look it up in a dictionary. Note: the dictionary lists words in the form they take for the **singular nominative**. In the examples we are looking at here they will all end in -ος (though not all Greek nouns do!).

- The case of the word (nominative, accusative, genitive or dative) and so what it is doing in the sentence.

- Whether it is singular or plural.

Try out these skills on the words in Table 4.2. You can find out the meaning using a dictionary, or one of the websites that have already been introduced.[1]

With a little practice, you should be able to recognize these endings instinctively. They are worth learning, because this is a core skill that will make you much more able to appreciate what's going on in the Greek.

Translating Nouns in Sentences

Here is a sentence taken from the Bible. The meaning of each Greek word is given underneath in English. By looking at the ending, work out if it is nominative, accusative, genitive and/or dative. Use this information to choose between the three possible translations provided. When you have made your choice, look up the passage in an English Bible to see if you are right:

Table 4.2

Word	Stem	Meaning	Nominative (N) Accusative (A) Genitive (G) or Dative (D)	Singular (S) or Plural (P)
θανατους				
θεον				
ἀγγελων				
κοσμου				
χριστῳ				
λογου				
νομοι				
υἱον				
ἀνθρωποις				
διαβολου				

ὅτε   δὲ ἐβλάστησεν ὁ χόρτος καὶ καρπὸν ἐποίησεν,

when but   sprouted the crop   and grain   made

(Matthew 13.26)

Possible translations:

(a) When he sprouted the crop and made grain
(b) When the grain sprouted and made a crop
(c) When the crop sprouted and made grain

χόρτος ('crop') is in the nominative case, so it is the subject: the crop is 'doing' something. καρπον ('grain') is in the accusative, so something is happening to it. The answer is (c), because the crop is making the grain.

You may have noticed that you discarded some options because their sense seemed obviously wrong. This is something that you will do regularly when reading the New Testament. It helps you narrow down the options as to the meaning of a sentence.

Practice at Translating Nouns in Sentences

Here are some more sentences with several possible translations. Try out your skills on each one:[2]

1   ἀποστελεῖ ὁ υἱὸς τοῦ ἀνθρώπου τοὺς ἀγγέλους αὐτοῦ,

    he-sent   the son the   man   the   angels   his

(Matthew 13.41)

Possible translations:

(a) The Son of Man sent his angels
(b) He sent his angels to the Son of Man
(c) Angels sent the man his son

2 τότε λέγει τῷ παραλυτικῷ·

Then he-says the   paralytic

(Matthew 9:6)

Possible translations:

   (a) Then the paralytic says

   (b) Then he says to the paralytic

Note: sometimes the subject of the sentence in English is a pronoun (I, you, he/she/it, they). In Greek, this is often not a separate word – it is merely indicated in the verb ending.

3 ἔλαβεν οὖν   τους ἄρτους ὁ Ἰησους

he-took therefore the   bread the Jesus

(John 6.11)

Possible translations:

   a) Therefore they took the bread from Jesus

   b) Therefore the bread took Jesus

   c) Therefore Jesus took the bread

THE WORD 'THE'

The Basics

If you look at the examples above, you will see that quite often the noun is preceded by a little word – ὁ, ἡ, οἱ, αἱ, or a word beginning with τ. This word is the 'definite article': always translated as 'the', although sometimes you will find that Greek uses the definite article where we do not, for example, 'Jesus' is written ὁ Ἰησοῦς, 'the Jesus'. If you think it would make better sense in English without the word 'the' then leave it out. If a noun has no definite article in front of it, we would normally translate it as 'a'. In English, the definite article never changes – the word 'the' is always written 'the' – but in Greek it does change.

Two things to look out for:

- **Number** (singular or plural): if the noun is singular (e.g. λογος) the definite article will be singular (e.g. ὁ λογος). If the noun is plural (e.g. λογοι), the definite article will be plural (οἱ λογοι).

- **Case** (nominative, accusative, genitive or dative): if the noun in the sentence is a nominative (e.g. ἀδελφος) the definite article will also be a nominative (e.g. ὁ ἀδελφος). If the noun is an accusative (e.g. ἀδελφον) so will the definite article be (e.g. τον ἀδελφον).

Table 4.3   Masculine Definite Article

Case	Singular Definite Article	Plural Definite Article
Nominative	ὁ	οἱ
Accusative	τον	τους
Possessive	του	των
Dative	τῳ	τοις

Look at Table 4.4. Each of the nouns on the right-hand side belong with one of the definite articles on the left. Identify which noun belongs with which article and write it in the space provided. The first one has been done for you.[3]

In addition to the changes with **case** and **number** (see above), the definite article also changes depending on the **gender** of the noun (see p. 54 for a discussion on gender). Knowing the gender of the definite article is useful, because it helps you to sort out which gender the noun is: if it has a definite article, the article will be the same gender as the noun. Look at the full chart of definite articles (Table 4.5).

Table 4.4

Definite Article	Your Answer	Noun
ὁ	διαβολος	λογοις
τον		ἀδελφου
του		διαβολος
τῳ		καρπον
οἱ		δουλῳ
τους		ἀγγελων
των		ἀποστολους
τοις		ἀνθρωποι

Table 4.5 is one of the most useful tools you will encounter in understanding Greek sentences. We suggest you photocopy it (either from here, or from the appendix) and make it into a card that you can refer to easily without having to flick backwards and forwards in the book. This will save a lot of time and effort when studying later chapters.

The reason Table 4.5 is so useful is because the endings of the definite article are always entirely consistent. Even though the endings of nouns may mislead you in various ways, where you have a noun with its definite article you will *always* be able to work out the case and number of the noun from the ending of its definite article.

You will *usually* be able to work out its gender as well, but you will see that some endings are the same for masculine and neuter nouns, and one (the genitive plural) is the same for all the genders. Fortunately, gender is relatively unimportant when reading the Greek New Testament.

It is worth noting two further ways in which the definite article is used in Greek:

Table 4.5

Singular	Masculine	Feminine	Neuter
Nominative	ὁ	ἡ	το
Accusative	τον	την	το
Genitive	του	της	του
Dative	τῳ	τη	τῳ
Plural			
Nominative	οἱ	αἱ	τα
Accusative	τους	τας	τα
Genitive	των	των	των
Dative	τοις	ταις	τοις

- Sometimes the definite article appears on its own without a noun. When it does this, it often refers back to a noun just mentioned and can be translated 'the one'.

- Sometimes Greek has two definite articles where we would have one. For example, ὁ λογος του θεου literally means 'the word of the god'. When you see something like this, translate the phrase with one article: 'the word of God'.

For example:

Τί   δὲ βλέπεις τὸ κάρφος   τὸ   ἐν τῷ ὀφθαλμῷ τοῦ

why but you-see the stalk   the-one in the   eye   of-the

ἀδελφοῦ σου;

brother of-you

(Luke 6.41)

This could be translated into English as:

> * Why do you see the stalk, the one in your brother's eye?

Practice Using Articles

Look at the following nouns with their articles. From the ending of the article, can you work out the gender of each noun? If the ending could belong to more than one gender indicate this in your answer.[4]

1 τους δουλους

2 ταις καρδιαις

3 τον ἀγγελον

4 τῳ ἀδελφῳ

5 αἱ γυναι

6 ταις ἡμεραις

7 των ἀρτων

8 της ἀρχης

9 την δοξαν

Identifying the Article in Bible Passages

In the following passages, underline the Greek word(s) for 'the' (omitted from the English translation) and the ending(s) of the noun(s) they refer to. You will notice that sometimes the ending of the noun is different from the ending of the definite article. Then answer the questions on each passage:[5]

1 Mark 1.14–15

ἦλθεν ὁ Ἰησοῦς εἰς τὴν Γαλιλαίαν κηρύσσων τὸ εὐαγγέλιον
he-came Jesus   into   Galilee   preaching   gospel

τοῦ θεοῦ καὶ λέγων ὅτι πεπλήρωται ὁ καιρὸς καὶ
of-God and saying that has-been-fulfilled   time   and

ἤγγικεν ἡ βασιλεία τοῦ θεοῦ· μετανοεῖτε καὶ
has-drawn-near kingdom   of-God. Repent and

πιστεύετε ἐν τῷ εὐαγγελίῳ.
believe in   gospel

(a) What case is τὴν Γαλιλαιαν?
(b) What gender is ἡ βασιλεια?

2 Matthew 6.5

Καὶ ὅταν προσεύχησθε, οὐκ ἔσεσθε ὡς οἱ ὑποκριταί,
And when you-pray, (do)-not be like hypocrites,

ὅτι φιλοῦσιν ἐν ταῖς συναγωγαῖς καὶ ἐν ταῖς γωνίαις
because they-love in   synagogues and in   corners

τῶν πλατειῶν ἑστῶτες προσεύχεσθαι, ὅπως φανῶσιν
   streets   standing   to-pray, so-that they-may-appear

τοῖς ἀνθρώποις· ἀμὴν λέγω ὑμῖν, ἀπέχουσιν τὸν μισθὸν
   people. Amen I-say to-you, they-have   reward

αὐτῶν.
their

(a) Give the number, gender and case of οἱ ὑποκριται.
(b) Give the number and case of των πλατειων. Why can't you
    tell its gender from this example?

THE THIRD PERSON PERSONAL PRONOUN

The last word in the passage above, αὐτων, is the genitive plural
of αὐτος. This means he/she/it and is a common and useful word
in Greek. Its forms are given in full in Table 4.6.

Table 4.6

Singular	Masculine	Feminine	Neuter	Meaning
Nominative	αὐτος	αὐτη	αὐτο	he / she / it
Accusative	αὐτον	αὐτην	αὐτο	him / her / it
Genitive	αὐτου	αυτης	αὐτου	his / hers / its
Dative	αὐτῳ	αὐτῃ	αὐτῳ	to him / to her / to it
Plural				
Nominative	αὐτοι	αὐται	αὐτα	they
Accusative	αὐτους	αὐτας	αὐτα	them
Genitive	αὐτων	αὐτων	αὐτων	theirs
Dative	αὐτοις	αὐταις	αὐτοις	to them

Notice that in English, for once, we also change the word according to its use in the sentence, and that in the singular we have different words for the different genders (masculine, feminine and neuter).

Compare the endings with the definite article. Do you notice any similarities between them?

Where does a form of αὐτος come in the following sentence? What case is it? Knowing this, which of the two translations offered is the right one?[6]

ἐκ τούτου   ὁ Πιλᾶτος ἐζήτει ἀπολῦσαι αὐτόν·

From   this   (time)   Pilate   sought to-release   he

(John 19.12)

Possible translations:

  (a) From then on, Pilate sought to set him free

  (b) From then on, he sought to release Pilate

As well as functioning as a personal pronoun (he, she, it), αὐτος can be used in two other ways, both of which are linked to a noun:

• The pronoun αὐτος can be used to emphasize a noun. For example, αὐτος ὁ Ἰησους or ὁ Ἰησους αὐτος means 'Jesus himself'.

• αὐτος can function as an adjective meaning 'the same'. For example, ὁ αὐτος λογος or ὁ λογος ὁ αὐτος means 'the same word'.

The formal distinction is that when used to emphasize a noun, αὐτος never separates the article and noun; and, when used to mean 'the same', αὐτος either separates an article and noun or takes its own article. Both uses are quite common in New Testament Greek but we will not study them in detail here.

More on Prepositions

In Chapter 2 we looked at prepositions and noticed that some of them change meaning depending on the case of the word that follows them.

So, for example, δια means 'on account of' if it is followed by an accusative but 'through' if it is followed by a genitive. A full chart of prepositions and their meanings is provided in the appendix to this book. You may find it helpful to glance at this occasionally to explain why certain prepositions seem to have different meanings on different occasions.

Have a look at the difference between these two examples:

1 John 17.20

I ask not only on behalf of these, but also on behalf of those who will believe in me **through their word,**

Οὐ περὶ τούτων δὲ ἐρωτῶ μόνον, ἀλλὰ καὶ περὶ τῶν πιστευόντων **διὰ τοῦ λόγου** αὐτῶν εἰς ἐμέ,

2 Matthew 13.21

yet such a person has no root, but endures only for a while, and when trouble or persecution arises **on account of the word**, that person immediately falls away.

οὐκ ἔχει δὲ ῥίζαν ἐν ἑαυτῷ ἀλλὰ πρόσκαιρος ἐστιν, γενομένης δὲ θλίψεως ἢ διωγμοῦ **διὰ τὸν λόγον** εὐθὺς σκανδαλίζεται.

Now you try. Find the relevant Greek preposition in Table A.1 of the appendix. Note the case of the noun it refers to, and use this information to fill in the gap in the English translation:

1 Romans 15.5

May the God of steadfastness and encouragement grant you to live in harmony with one another, ... Christ Jesus,

ὁ δὲ θεὸς τῆς ὑπομονῆς καὶ τῆς παρακλήσεως δῴη ὑμῖν τὸ αὐτὸ φρονεῖν ἐν ἀλλήλοις **κατὰ** Χριστὸν Ἰησοῦν,

2 Acts 4.26

The kings of the earth took their stand, and the rulers have gathered together . . . . the Lord and . . . . his Messiah.

παρέστησαν οἱ βασιλεῖς τῆς γῆς καὶ οἱ ἄρχοντες συνήχθησαν ἐπὶ τὸ αὐτὸ **κατὰ** τοῦ κυρίου καὶ **κατὰ** τοῦ χριστοῦ αὐτοῦ.

Further Practice with Cases, Articles and Pronouns

Go to *The Online Greek Bible* website www.greekbible.com.[7]

- In the boxes after the word 'Passage:' select Romans 2.16 and click 'go'. You will now see the passage in Greek.

- If you click on a Greek word, a window will open giving the meaning. In most cases, it will also give you a little box. For nouns, the box will tell you the case, number and gender. Identify the nouns in this passage (you may find it helpful to refer to an English translation) and write down the case, number and gender of each.

- Alternatively, look up the words in a Greek–English dictionary. To do this, you will need to work out the stem for each one. You will find that some of the endings are kinds that you haven't come across so far. Make a note of these to refer back to when you study the next chapter.

REVIEW OF LEARNING

In this chapter we have looked at:

- nouns and their cases: nominative, accusative, genitive and dative;
- the definite article;
- the third person personal pronoun;
- some more on prepositions.

Notes

1 Your table should look like this:

Word	Stem	Meaning	Nominative (N) Accusative (A) Genitive (G) or Dative (D)	Singular (S) or Plural (P)
θανατους	θανατ-	death	A	P
θεον	θε-	God	A	S
ἀγγελων	αγγελ-	angel	G	P
κοσμου	κοσμ-	world	G	S
χριστω	χριστ-	Christ	D	S
λογου	λογ-	word	G	S
νομοι	νομ-	law	N	P
υἱον	υἱ-	son	A	S
ἀνθρωποις	ἀνθρωπ-	man	D	P
διαβολου	διαβολ-	devil	G	S

2 (1) a; (2) b; (3) c.
3 The words that go together are: ὁ διαβολος, τον καρπον, του ἀδελφου, τῳ δουλῳ, οἱ ἀνθρωποι, τους ἀποστολους, των ἀγγελων, τοις λογοις.
4 (1) masculine; (2) feminine; (3) masculine; (4) masculine or neuter; (5) feminine; (6) feminine; (7) masculine, feminine or neuter; (8) feminine; (9) feminine.
5 (1a) accusative; (1b) feminine; (2a) plural, masculine, nominative; (2b) plural, genitive. We can't tell the gender because all genitive plurals have the same ending.
6 The form of αὐτος in this sentence is αὐτον. It's in the accusative, so means 'him'.
7 ἡμερα (dative, singular, feminine); θεος (nominative, singular, masculine); ἀνθρωπων (genitive, plural, masculine); εὐαγγελιον (accusative, singular, neuter); χριστου (genitive, singular, masculine) Ἰησους (genitive, singular, masculine).

5

More Noun Endings and More Pronouns

MORE NOUN ENDINGS

In the last chapter, we began to look at nouns and their endings and to notice how the ending of the noun sometimes matched the ending of the definite article that it went with, for example, τοις λογοις.

When you were reading Greek passages from the Bible in the previous chapters, you will have noticed that not all noun endings look like those for λογος:

- Some noun endings still match their definite article but with different letters in the ending (e.g. ἡ ἀρχη, or της ἀρχης). In this case the endings are matching the feminine definite article (telling us incidentally that the noun is feminine).

- Other noun endings bear no resemblance at all to the definite article that goes with them (e.g. του πατρος). These are the trickiest kind of nouns to identify.

Nouns that Match their Definite Article

The noun endings that we looked at in the last chapter had endings similar to the masculine definite article. Other types of nouns have endings that are similar to the feminine article and to the neuter article. These nouns take the forms shown in Table 5.1.

Table 5.1

Singular	Feminine	Feminine	Feminine	Neuter
Nominative	ἀρχη	καρδια	δοξα	ἐργον
Accusative	ἀρχην	καρδιαν	δοξαν	ἐργον
Genitive	ἀρχης	καρδιας	δοξης	ἐργου
Dative	ἀρχῃ	καρδιᾳ	δοξῃ	ἐργῳ
Plural				
Nominative	ἀρχαι	καρδιαι	δοξαι	ἐργα
Accusative	ἀρχας	καρδιας	δοξας	ἐργα
Genitive	ἀρχων	καρδιων	δοξων	ἐργων
Dative	ἀρχαις	καρδιαις	δοξαις	ἐργοις

If you compare Table 5.1 with the definite article table (Table 4.5) you will notice that the endings of ἀρχη are exactly the same as those for the feminine definite article; the endings of καρδια and δοξα are similar to the feminine definite article but with some differences; and the endings of ἐργον are similar to the neuter article. Where there are differences, they are not big enough to make it difficult to recognize that the article and noun go together. For example, the endings of την δοξαν or το ἐργον are close enough for us easily to recognize that they fit together.

These different endings are not randomly applied to the nouns but follow these rules:

1 All the nouns that are listed in the dictionary as ending with -ος in their singular subject (or nominative) form will have endings like λογος.

2 All those ending with -ον will have endings like ἐργον.

3 All those ending with -η, will have endings like ἀρχη.

4 All those ending with ρ or a vowel followed by -α will have endings like καρδια

5 All those ending with a consonant followed by an -α will have endings like δοξα.

Numbers 1 and 2 are sometimes called second declension nouns and numbers 3 to 5 are sometimes called first declension nouns.

Based on these rules, give the correct form of the nouns in Table 5.2, making sure that you follow the right pattern for each noun. You may never want to translate from English into Greek, but by doing this you will grow familiar with some of the common forms. The first one has been done for you.[1]

Table 5.2

Noun – as it would appear in the dictionary	Put it into this form	Your answer
ἀκοη (hearing)	accusative singular	ἀκοην
ζωη (life)	accusative plural	
παιδιον (child)	genitive plural	
διαβολος (slanderer or devil)	genitive singular	
θαλασσα (sea)	genitive plural	
θεος (god)	nominative plural	
οἰκια (house)	dative singular	
βιβλιον (book)	accusative singular	
ἡμερα (day)	accusative plural	
γραφη (a writing)	dative plural	

Now look at the following and, as you did in the previous chapter, identify the correct translation for each verse. Common words you should know by now have been left untranslated:[2]

1 ὁ δὲ θεὸς γινώσκει τὰς καρδίας ὑμῶν·

    God   knows   hearts   your

(Luke 16.15)

Possible translations:

(a) But God knows your hearts.

(b) But you know God in your hearts.

(c) But your hearts know God.

2 Ἐὰν ταῖς γλώσσαις τῶν ἀνθρώπων λαλῶ καὶ τῶν ἀγγέλων,

    If   tongues   people   I-speak   angels,

ἀγάπην δὲ μὴ ἔχω,   γέγονα   χαλκὸς ἠχῶν ἢ κύμβαλον

    love   I-have, I-have-become brass echoing or   cymbal

ἀλαλάζον.

    tinkling

(1 Corinthians 13.1)

Possible translations:

(a) If the tongues of the people speak of angels but I do not have love, I am an echoing brass or a tinkling cymbal.

(b) If I speak in the tongues of the people and of the angels but I have not love, I am an echoing brass or a tinkling cymbal.

(c) If I speak in the tongues of people and do not have love for the angels, I am an echoing brass or a tinkling cymbal.

3 τότε λέγει τοῖς μαθηταῖς αὐτοῦ

then   says   disciples

(Matthew 9.37)

Note: 'disciples' is an unusual noun in Greek. Don't look at the noun ending, but look at the definite article.

Possible translations:

(a) Then the disciples say to him

(b) Then he says to the disciples

(c) Then he says to his disciples

Nouns that Do Not Match their Definite Article

Have a look at number 3 again. Do you notice anything strange about τοῖς μαθηταῖς?

Given its ending, you may expect μαθηταις to take the feminine definite article. However, there are a few nouns that take feminine endings that are, in fact, masculine and so take a masculine definite article. Similarly, a few nouns that take endings like λογος are feminine and will appear with a feminine definite article. This is not important but is worth knowing because it might confuse you if you are unaware of it.

The nouns that look masculine but are feminine and those that look feminine but are masculine differ from their definite article only in a minor way. However, there are other nouns which end up looking very different from their definite article, for example:

το σωμα, ἡ πολις and ὁ πατηρ

These bear very little resemblance either to the definite article or to any of the other nouns that we have just looked at. You will find these called third declension nouns in some books.

Most of the time you will be able to work out the number, gender and case of the noun in the sentence either from the definite article that comes with it or from the context.

Look at the following sentences and answer the questions after each:[3]

1   ὁ τρώγων μου τὴν σάρκα καὶ πίνων   μου τὸ αἷμα
the-one eating of-me the flesh and drinking of-me the blood

ἔχει ζωὴν αἰώνιον,
has life eternal

(John 6.54)

From the definite articles that go before them and from the context of the sentence, can you work out the case (nominative, accusative, genitive or dative) of σάρκα and αἷμα and whether they are singular or plural?

2 Τότε παραλαμβάνει αὐτὸν ὁ διάβολος εἰς τὴν ἁγίαν πόλιν
then took   he the devil   into the holy   city

(Matthew 4.5)

Is πόλιν nominative, accusative, genitive or dative and singular or plural?

3 ἀναστὰς πορεύσομαι πρὸς τὸν πατέρα μου καὶ ἐρῶ αὐτῷ·
getting-up I-will-travel to the father my and I-will-say he

(Luke 15.18)

What about πατέρα? Is it nominative, accusative, genitive or dative and singular or plural?

This should show you that if you know the definite article (or have a chart of it to hand) you can normally work out the rest of what you need to know without worrying too much about how it gets there.

However, sometimes the definite article is not present and then you have to try and work out what the noun is doing in other ways.

If you look at Table 5.3 you will begin to see the problem with this type of noun.

Table 5.3

Singular

Nominative	ἀστηρ	πατηρ	σωμα	γενος	ἰχθυς	πολις	βασιλευς
Accusative	ἀστερα	πατερα	σωμα	γενος	ἰχθυν	πολιν	βασιλεα
Genitive	ἀστερος	πατρος	σωματος	γενους	ἰχθυος	πολεως	βασιλεως
Dative	ἀστερι	πατρι	σωματι	γενει	ἰχθυι	πολει	βασιλει

Plural

Nominative	ἀστερες	πατερες	σωματα	γενη	ἰχθυες	πολεις	βασιλεις
Accusative	ἀστερας	πατερας	σωματα	γενη	ἰχθυας	πολεις	βασιλεις
Genitive	ἀστερων	πατερων	σωματων	γενων	ἰχθυων	πολεων	βασιλεων
Dative	ἀστερσιν	πατρασιν	σωμασιν	γενεσιν	ἰχθυσιν	πολεσιν	βασιλευσιν

Not only are the endings different from those we are used to, even the form of the noun changes.

If you look at πατηρ in Table 5.3 you will notice that in the nominative form it has a long η before the ρ. In the accusative singular, and nominative, accusative and genitive plural it has a short ε but in the genitive singular, dative singular and dative plural it has no ε or η at all.

Really, the only way to be certain to recognize the forms of this type of noun is to learn all the endings above. As you are unlikely either to want to or to have the time to do this you will have to acknowledge that sometimes when this type of noun occurs without its definite article you will simply have to work out from the context what it means, guess what function it is playing, or rely on a website or interlinear Bible to tell you.

There are a few tips that might help you a little:

- The genitive plural (as with all other types of noun) ends in -ων. You should always be able to tell this.

- All dative singulars of this type end in -ι. Again this might help you to work it out.

- All dative plurals end in –σιν.

Other than this there is very little pattern to be found, but before you despair, remember that this type of noun doesn't occur very often without a definite article.

Have a go at working out the following sentences and see how possible it is to guess! You can check your answers by calling up the verse on *The Online Greek Bible* website (www. greekbible.com) and clicking on the word you want to find out about:[4]

1 καὶ ὅπου ἄν   εἰσεπορεύετο εἰς κώμας ἢ εἰς πόλεις ἢ

   and wherever   he-went   into villages or into cities or

εἰς ἀγρούς

into fields   (Mark 6.56)

Look at πόλεις. Can you work out whether it is nominative, accusative, genitive or dative? (**Tip:** notice that 'villages' and 'fields' are the other types of noun, first and second declension respectively. Work out what they are and you have the case of cities!)

2   ὁ   ἀφορίσας   με   ἐκ   κοιλίας   μητρός   μου

  the-one   setting-apart me from womb   mother   of-me

(Galatians 1.15)

Look at μητρος. Is it nominative, accusative, genitive or dative? (**Tip:** there is really only one way of translating this into English.)

3 καὶ ἰδοὺ ἄνθρωπος χεῖρα ἔχων ξηράν

  and behold   a-man   a-hand having withered

(Matthew 12.10)

Look at χεῖρα. Is it nominative, accusative, genitive or dative? (**Tip:** again, there's not much else this can mean in English.)

The moral of this is that you should not feel ashamed about using an interlinear New Testament, a website or a computer program to help you work out the meaning of a word. This course aims to teach you to use tools you have to hand to read the Greek New Testament – so use them and don't feel it's cheating!

In the following sentences indicate which you think is the correct translation. Words you should know have been left untranslated:[5]

1 ὥσπερ γὰρ ἡ γυνὴ ἐκ τοῦ ἀνδρός, οὕτως καὶ ὁ ἀνὴρ διὰ τῆς

  Just as   woman   man, so-also   man

  γυναικός·

  woman

(1 Corinthians 11.12)

Note: you may have noticed there is no verb in this sentence! Greek can do this but we need to put in a verb that will make sense of it. The NRSV suggests 'came' here.

Possible translations:

(a) For just as from the woman came the man, so also the man comes through the woman.

(b) For just as the woman came from the man, so also the man comes through the woman.

(c) For just as the woman came from the man, so also the woman comes through the man.

You will have noticed that this sentence is made up of two clauses, each with its own subject and object. In each clause, the object is not in the accusative case. This is because some prepositions have to be followed by a noun in some other case. So, in this example, ἐκ and δια both take the genitive case.

2   εἴδομεν   γὰρ αὐτοῦ τὸν ἀστέρα ἐν τῇ ἀνατολῇ καὶ

we-have-seen   star   east

    ἤλθομεν   προσκυνῆσαι αὐτῷ.

we-have-come   to-worship

(Matthew 2.2)

Possible translations:

(a) For we have seen him in the Eastern star and we have come to worship it.

(b) For the star has seen him in the East and we have come to worship him.

(c) For we have seen his star in the East and have come to worship him.

Note: the last word is the dative, αὐτῷ rather than the accusative, αὐτον. In Greek, they 'worship *to* him'.

Even if you know which is the right one without working it out, can you say why it is right?

3 ἀμὴν ἀμὴν λέγω ὑμῖν, ἐὰν μὴ φάγητε τὴν σάρκα τοῦ υἱοῦ

         I-say to-you unless you-eat   flesh   son

τοῦ ἀνθρώπου καὶ πίητε αὐτοῦ τὸ αἷμα, οὐκ ἔχετε   ζωὴν

      man   drink   blood   you-do-have   life

ἐν ἑαυτοῖς.

    you

(John 6.53)

Possible translations:

(a) Truly, truly I say to you unless you eat of the flesh of the Son of Man and drink of his blood, you do not have life in you.

(b) Truly, truly I say to you unless you eat the flesh of the Son of Man and drink his blood, you do not have life in you.

(c) Truly, truly I say to you unless you eat the Son of Man and his flesh and drink his blood, you do not have life in you.

Again can you say why the one you have chosen is right?

4 μισθὸν οὐκ ἔχετε παρὰ τῷ πατρὶ ὑμῶν τῷ ἐν τοῖς οὐρανοῖς.

reward   you-have from   father your   heavens

(Matthew 6.1)

Possible translations:

(a) You do not have a reward from your father in the heavens.

(b) Your reward does not have a father in the heavens.

(c) Your father in the heavens does not have your reward.

MORE PRONOUNS

Personal Pronouns

We have already met the third person pronoun αὐτος. Now we are going to look at the others. As soon as you see them you will probably recognize them because they come up so often in the Greek text.

The remaining ordinary pronouns are the **first** and **second person pronoun** in both singular and plural (Table 5.4). You will notice that they are quite different from each other and sometimes look a little bit like the third declension nouns above.

Table 5.4

	1st Person Singular	Meaning	2nd Person Singular	Meaning
Nominative	ἐγω		συ	
Accusative	ἐμε (με)		σε	
Genitive	ἐμου (μου)		σου	
Dative	ἐμοι (μοι)		σοι	
	1st Person Plural	Meaning	2nd Person Plural	Meaning
Nominative	ἡμεις		ὑμεις	
Accusative	ἡμας		ὑμας	
Genitive	ἡμων		ὑμων	
Dative	ἡμιν		ὑμιν	

Note: in the accusative, genitive and dative of the first person pronoun singular, there are two possible forms of the word ἐμε or με. The form in brackets is the alternative form. There is no real difference between these and you will find both forms in the Greek text.

Look at the following Bible verses which use the first and second person pronouns singular and plural and fill in the meanings of each pronoun in the relevant column in Table 5.4.[6]

1 ἐγὼ ἀπέστειλα ὑμᾶς θερίζειν ὃ   οὐχ ὑμεῖς κεκοπιάκατε

   I   I-sent   you   to-reap what not you   sowed

   * I sent you to reap what you did not sow. (John 4.38)

2   Ὁ   δεχόμενος ὑμᾶς ἐμὲ δέχεται

   the-one receiving   you me receives

   * The one who receives you, receives me. (Matthew 10.40)

3 σὺ   εἶ   ὁ υἱός μου ὁ   ἀγαπητός, ἐν σοὶ

   you you-are the son of-me the beloved-one in you

   εὐδόκησα.

   I-am-well-pleased

   * You are my beloved son, with you I am well pleased. (Mark 1.11)

Note: remember that the dative can be used on its own, meaning 'to', 'by', 'with' or 'for' something or someone; or with a preposition, when it takes the meaning of the preposition. The preposition ἐν (in) here means that the phrase ἐν σοι is translated 'in you'.

4 τήρησον αὐτοὺς ἐν τῷ ὀνόματι σου   ᾧ   δέδωκας

   guard   them in the name of-you which you-have-given

   μοι, ἵνα   ὦσιν   ἓν καθὼς ἡμεῖς.

   to-me so-that they-might-be one as   we (are one)

   * Protect them in your name that you have given me, so that they
   may be one, as we are one. (John 17.11)

Note: ἓν is different from ἐν (see third and fourth passages). If
you look carefully you will see that ἓν has an accent over it and
a hard or rough breathing but ἐν has no accent and a soft breathing. These marks are important as ἓν means 'one' and ἐν means
'in'. Look out for these or you will get confused!

5 Καὶ ἐὰν σκανδαλίζῃ   σε ἡ χείρ σου,

   and if causes-to-stumble you the hand of-you

   * If your hand causes you to stumble, (Mark 9.43)

6   ἦλθες   ἀπολέσαι ἡμᾶς; οἶδα σε τίς εἶ, ὁ

   you-have-come to-destroy us? I-know you who you-are the

   ἅγιος   τοῦ θεοῦ.

   holy-one of-the God

   * Have you come to destroy us? I know who you are, the Holy One
   of God. (Luke 4.34)

Note: you will have noticed in these examples that sometimes a
verb comes *with* a pronoun (e.g. συ εἶ in passage 3 translates
as 'you who you-are') and sometimes a verb occurs on its own
without a pronoun, (e.g. in the same passage, the verb δέδωκας
means 'you-have-given'). This is because, unlike in English, in

Greek you do not need a pronoun because the ending of the verb tells you everything you need to know (as we will see in Chapter 7 onwards). Sometimes, however, the author wants to stress who he is talking about. When that happens he puts in the pronoun so we are left in no doubt.

7 τὸν ἄρτον ἡμῶν τὸν ἐπιούσιον δὸς ἡμῖν σήμερον·

the bread of-us the   daily   give to-us today

* Give us this day our daily bread. (Matthew 6.11)

8 ἔστω δὲ   ὁ λόγος ὑμῶν ναὶ ναί, οὒ οὔ·

let-be but the word of-you yes yes no no

* Let your word be 'Yes, Yes' or 'No, No'. (Matthew 5.37)

9 ἐγὼ δὲ λέγω ὑμῖν

I   but I-say to-you

* But I say to you (Matthew 5.22)

Look at the following Greek passage. Don't worry about trying to translate or even understand it but see how many pronouns you can find in it. Check your answers with an English Bible if you like:[7]

Ἐφανέρωσά σου τὸ ὄνομα τοῖς ἀνθρώποις οὓς ἔδωκάς μοι ἐκ τοῦ κόσμου. σοὶ ἦσαν καμοὶ αὐτοὺς ἔδωκας καὶ τὸν λόγον σου τετήρηκαν. νῦν ἔγνωκαν ὅτι πάντα ὅσα δέδωκάς μοι παρὰ σοῦ εἰσιν· ὅτι τὰ ῥήματα ἃ ἔδωκάς μοι δέδωκα αὐτοῖς, καὶ αὐτοὶ ἔλαβον καὶ ἔγνωσαν ἀληθῶς ὅτι παρὰ σοῦ ἐξῆλθον, καὶ ἐπίστευσαν ὅτι σύ με ἀπέστειλας. Ἐγὼ περὶ αὐτῶν ἐρωτῶ, οὐ περὶ τοῦ κόσμου ἐρωτῶ ἀλλὰ περὶ ὧν δέδωκάς μοι, ὅτι σοί εἰσιν

(John 17.6–9)

Reflexive Pronouns

In addition to these simple personal pronouns you will also occasionally come across pronouns that we call **reflexive pronouns**. These are translated with the word 'self' at the end (myself, yourself, herself, etc.) They are formed by adding:

* ἐμ to the start of αὐτος (with the right ending) for myself/ourselves;

* σε to the start of αὐτος (with the right ending) for yourself;

* ἑ to the start of αὐτος (with the right ending) for himself, themselves.

Similarly, feminine reflexive pronouns are formed by adding ἐμ, σε or ἑ to the feminine form αὐτη.

These are easily recognizable from the beginning of the word, so we do not need to study them in detail here. To see how they work in practice look at the following examples:

1 ἐὰν ἐγὼ   δοξάσω   ἐμαυτόν, ἡ δόξα μου   οὐδέν ἐστιν·

   if   I I-were-to-glorify myself the glory of-me nothing is

   * If I glorify myself, my glory is nothing. (John 8.54)

2   τί   λέγεις   περὶ σεαυτοῦ;

   what do-you-say about yourself

   * What do you say about yourself? (John 1.22)

3 ἄφες τοὺς νεκροὺς θάψαι τοὺς   ἑαυτῶν   νεκρούς.

   allow the   dead to-bury the of-themselves dead

   * Let the dead bury their own dead. (Matthew 8.22)

LOOKING AT TRANSLATIONS OF GREEK PASSAGES

One of the aims of this Greek course is to help you to use a Greek New Testament alongside other English translations so that you can see the advantages and disadvantages of each translation. There is no such thing as a perfect translation: it is good to stay as close as possible to the Greek, but there are other factors to take into consideration. For example, we may want a translation that is easy to understand in the modern world, or one that we think explains the original intention of the author clearly, or one that expands our understanding of the text rather than limiting it.

From this point in the course onwards we will look at passages (of increasing length) alongside different published translations of the Bible, exploring what we feel is the 'best' translation. The translation that is 'best' for academic study may not be the best for Bible study or personal devotion, so there is no one right answer to our question. But by studying the original Greek we will learn how to give reasons why we might prefer one translation over another.

Look at the following sentence:

[καὶ] λέγει αὐτῇ ὁ Ἰησοῦς· τί ἐμοὶ καὶ σοί, γύναι; οὔπω
and he-says she the Jesus what I   and you woman? Not-yet

ἥκει   ἡ ὥρα μου.
has-come the hour I

(John 2.4)

Given the work we have done on pronouns in this chapter look carefully at αὐτῇ, ἐμοι, σοι and μου and make sure you can work out what their ending is and how they should be translated.

Now look at the following translations and see what you think about them:

And Jesus said to her, 'Woman, what concern is that to you and to me? My hour has not yet come.' (NRSV)

'Dear woman, why do you involve me?' Jesus replied. 'My time has not yet come.' (NIV)

Jesus answered, 'Dear woman, why come to me? My time has not yet come.' (NCV)

Go through each translation carefully and ask:

• What words has each one added – how justifiable is this?

• What words have been missed out – again, how justifiable is this?

• What tone does each give to the sentence – is it different between translations?

• Which one do you prefer and why?

• Do you want to alter any part of your preferred translation in the light of what the Greek says?

You may like to know that:

• the question 'what to me and to you' could be either aggressive or peaceful.

• It is highly unusual to address your mother as 'woman' but is not necessarily aggressive.

REVIEW OF LEARNING

In this chapter we have looked at:

• more noun endings that match their definite article;

• noun endings that don't match their definite article;

- first and second person personal pronouns;
- reflexive pronouns;
- beginning to explore different biblical translations.

Notes

1 ζωας, παιδιων, διαβολου, θαλασσων, θεοι, οἰκιᾳ, βιβλιον, ἡμερας, γραφαις.
2 (1) a; (2) b; (3) c.
3 (1) Both nouns are accusative singular, (2) πόλιν is accusative singular, (3) πατέρα is accusative singular.
4 (1) πόλεις is accusative, (2) μητρός is genitive, (3) χεῖρα is accusative.
5 (1) b; (2) c, τὸν ἀστέρα (star) is accusative and is therefore what is being seen; (3) b, τὴν σάρκα (flesh) is accusative and is therefore what is being eaten, τοῦ υἱοῦ τοῦ ἀνθρώπου (of the Son of Man) is genitive, indicating that the Son of Man possesses what is being eaten; (4) a.
6 Your table should look like this:

	1st Person Singular	Meaning	2nd Person Singular	Meaning
Nominative	ἐγω	I	συ	you
Accusative	ἐμε (με)	me	σε	you
Genitive	ἐμου (μου)	of me, my	σου	of you, your
Dative	ἐμοι (μοι)	to me	σοι	to you

	1st Person Plural	Meaning	2nd Person Plural	Meaning
Nominative	ἡμεις	we	ὑμεις	you
Accusative	ἡμας	us	ὑμας	you
Genitive	ἡμων	of us, our	ὑμων	of you, your
Dative	ἡμιν	to us	ὑμιν	to you

7 Ἐφανέρωσα <u>σου</u> τὸ ὄνομα τοῖς ἀνθρώποις οὓς ἔδωκας <u>μοι</u> ἐκ τοῦ κόσμου. <u>σοὶ</u> ἦσαν καμοὶ <u>αὐτοὺς</u> ἔδωκας καὶ τὸν λόγον <u>σου</u> τετήρηκαν. νῦν ἔγνωκαν ὅτι πάντα ὅσα δέδωκας <u>μοι</u> παρὰ <u>σοῦ</u> εἰσιν· ὅτι τὰ ῥήματα ἃ ἔδωκας <u>μοι</u> δέδωκα <u>αὐτοῖς</u>, καὶ <u>αὐτοὶ</u> ἔλαβον καὶ ἔγνωσαν ἀληθῶς ὅτι παρὰ <u>σοῦ</u> ἐξῆλθον, καὶ ἐπίστευσαν ὅτι <u>σύ</u> <u>με</u> ἀπέστειλας. Ἐγὼ περὶ <u>αὐτῶν</u> ἐρωτῶ, οὐ περὶ τοῦ κόσμου ἐρωτῶ ἀλλὰ περὶ ὧν δέδωκας <u>μοι</u>, ὅτι <u>σοί</u> εἰσιν, (John 17.6–9).

6

Words that Describe

In Chapters 4 and 5 we focused on nouns – words that name a person, place or thing. In this chapter we will focus on words that describe the noun:

- adjectives, which can be used in a range of ways;
- demonstratives – 'this' and 'that';
- relative pronouns – 'who' and 'which'.

In addition, we will briefly look at adverbs – words that describe the action in a sentence.

ADJECTIVES

Adjectives behave in a very similar way to the definite article and nouns. They can be used to describe, to assert and to stand in place of nouns. In what follows we shall explore how to recognize adjectives and how their meaning changes depending on their function in a sentence.

The Basic Rules

The basic use of an adjective in Greek is to tell you more about a noun. In English, the word order tells us which noun the adjective is referring to: the adjective usually comes immediately before the noun or after the word 'is' (e.g. 'the old house is big'). But as you know, in Greek the word order is much less important: we recognize how a word fits into a sentence from its ending. We know when an adjective and a noun 'belong' together because their endings show that they have the same case, number and gender.

Because an adjective can be used with a masculine, feminine or neuter noun, it has to have three sets of endings, one for each gender. In the dictionary you will usually find the nominative singular masculine form with the nominative singular endings for the feminine and neuter forms, for example, ἀγαθος -η -ον, which means 'good'. As with the definite article, this will mean that sometimes the ending of an adjective will look exactly like its definite article and noun but sometimes it will not.

For example:

καὶ ἕτερον ἔπεσεν εἰς **τὴν γῆν τὴν ἀγαθὴν**

and another   fell   into **the earth the good**

(Luke 8.8)

Here the ending of 'good' looks the same as the endings of both the definite article and the noun 'earth'.

But look at this verse:

Μαριὰμ γὰρ **τὴν ἀγαθὴν μερίδα** ἐξελέξατο

Mary   for **the good part** has-chosen

(Luke 10.42)

Here the ending of 'good' looks the same as the ending of the definite article but different from the ending of the noun 'part'.

In fact both nouns are feminine, accusative singular but are different types of noun (γην is like ἀρχη, but μερίδα is one of those third declension nouns we looked at in the last chapter whose endings do not match the definite article). Adjectives will always match the noun they are with in case, number and gender but may not always look as though they are doing so.

As with the more complex types of noun, you should be able

to work out the ending of the adjective from the definite article (if it is present).

Table 6.1 shows you the endings for most adjectives (κακος -η -ον means 'evil' or 'bad').

Table 6.1

	Masculine	Feminine	Neuter
Singular			
Nominative	κακος	κακη	κακον
Accusative	κακον	κακην	κακον
Genitive	κακου	κακης	κακου
Dative	κακῳ	κακῃ	κακῳ
Plural			
Nominative	κακοι	κακαι	κακα
Accusative	κακους	κακας	κακα
Genitive	κακων	κακων	κακων
Dative	κακοις	κακαις	κακοις

Spend a moment comparing Table 6.1 with Table 4.5 for the definite article and noting the similarities of the endings.

Note: adjectives whose stem ends in a ρ or a vowel, for example, ἁγιος -α -ον, have slightly different endings when used to describe a feminine noun. They are the same as the endings for καρδια, which we encountered in Chapter 5.

At first sight the very common adjective πας -α -αν seems irregular (in fact in the masculine and neuter it follows the form of some of the third declension nouns) and is worth glancing at in its full form in Table 6.2.

Table 6.2

	Masculine	Feminine	Neuter
Singular			
Nominative	πας	πασα	παν
Accusative	παντα	πασαν	παν
Genitive	παντος	πασης	παντος
Dative	παντι	παση	παντι
Plural			
Nominative	παντες	πασαι	παντα
Accusative	παντας	πασας	παντα
Genitive	παντων	πασων	παντων
Dative	πασι(ν)	πασαις	πασι(ν)

Note: the dative plural πασι is sometimes written πασιν, so we have put the ν in brackets. It means exactly the same thing.

The word πας has come over into many English words, for example, panoply, pantheism, panorama. Can you work out what it means from these examples? Check your answer in a dictionary or website.

Adjectives and the Definite Article

As you already know, in English we signify that words belong together (like nouns, adjectives and definite articles) by putting them in a particular order. In Greek, words that belong together share the same case, number and gender, which can be worked out from their endings.

This means the word order in Greek can be much more flexible. Thus 'a good prophet' could be written ἀγαθος προφητης or προφητης ἀγαθος but would mean the same whatever order it came in.

When we want to say '*the* good prophet', the definite article is needed as well. Note however that the adjective must have a definite article *directly* in front of it wherever it appears in relation to the noun, so ὁ ἀγαθος προφητης and ὁ προφητης ὁ ἀγαθος both mean 'the good prophet'.

In the first example the adjective has the definite article in front of it anyway so doesn't need another one in front of the noun. In the second example the adjective has the noun between it and the definite article so it needs another definite article in front of it.

Look at the sentences below. The adjectives, and the nouns they go with, are all in bold. Go through them and circle the definite articles that go with them. Notice where the definite articles are and how many of them there are (in other words if the adjective is first there is one article, if second there are two).

When you have done this, practise putting the sentences into good English – you can check your answers in your English translation.[1]

1 Ἐγώ εἰμι ἡ **ἄμπελος** ἡ **ἀληθινὴ**

  I   I-am the **vine** the **true**

(John 15.1)

2 ἐὰν δὲ   εἴπῃ   ὁ **κακὸς δοῦλος** ἐκεῖνος ἐν τῇ

  if   but he-should-say the **wicked slave**   that   in the

καρδίᾳ αὐτοῦ·

heart   his

(Matthew 24.48)

3 ἵνα   στρατεύῃ ἐν αὐταῖς τὴν **καλὴν στρατείαν**

  so-that you-might-fight in   them the **good**   **fight**

(1 Timothy 1.18)

Adjectives also often appear without definite articles. Here are some examples:

1 ἐν καρδίᾳ καλῇ καὶ ἀγαθῇ

   in   heart   fine and good

(Luke 8.15)

2 πολλὰ ἔργα καλὰ   ἔδειξα   ὑμῖν ἐκ τοῦ πατρός·

  many works good I-have-shown to-you from the   father

(John 10.32)

Notice that in both examples the adjectives are paired; Greek often does this. Also note the adjective πολλα. This is from πολυς, πολλη, πολυ, which is another very common irregular adjective, meaning 'much' or 'many'.

3 συνείδησιν ἔχοντες ἀγαθήν

  conscience having   good

(1 Peter 3.16)

Note that adjectives can be split from their noun in Greek! Here the noun and adjective are either side of the verb – but we know they are connected because their endings match.

More Ways to Use Adjectives

As well as being used to describe nouns (sometimes called the attributive use), adjectives can also be used in two other ways:

  1 When they appear on their own, with or without a definite article, they function as a noun (this is sometimes called the pronominal use). For example:

    ὁ ἀγαθος   the good (man)

ἀγαθαι   good (women)

τα ἀγαθα   the good (things)

Often (though not always) in English we have to add an extra
word here to make the noun make sense. Generally speaking
we can add either 'one/ones', 'man/men' or 'woman/women'
depending on the gender, number and context. Note from the
examples above that there could be instances when you would
not want to add anything. For example, the phrase 'the good' has
a meaning of its own without anything more.

Look at the following sentences and compare them to the text
of the same reading in your English Bible. What word(s) have to
be added to the translations below in order for them to make
sense in English? The adjective is marked in bold to make it
easier for you. Again you can check the sentence in your English
Bible to see if you are right.[2]

1 μὴ   μιμοῦ   τὸ κακὸν ἀλλὰ **τὸ ἀγαθόν**

not do-imitate the   bad   but **the   good**

(3 John 11)

2 καὶ   καθίσαντες   συνέλεξαν   **τὰ καλὰ** εἰς ἄγγη

and having-sat-down they-collected **the good** into baskets

(Matthew 13.48)

2 When there is a definite article before the noun, but no
definite article directly before the adjective you need to supply
the verb 'to be' (this is sometimes called the predicative use).
Thus, both ἀγαθος ὁ προφητης and ὁ προφητης ἀγαθος mean
'the prophet is good'.

Table 6.3 summarizes the different ways in which an adjective
can be used.

Check that you understand the different uses of an adjective
by working out what the following mean. καλον means 'good',

Table 6.3

ἀγαθος προφητης or προφητης ἀγαθος = a good prophet	ὁ ἀγαθος προφητης or ὁ προφητης ὁ ἀγαθος = the good prophet
(ὁ) ἀγαθος = a/the good	ἀγαθος ὁ προφητης or ὁ προφητης ἀγαθος = the prophet is good

'fine' or 'beautiful' and παιδιον means 'child'. (Some of the phrases below have the same meaning and should be translated the same way!)[3]

το καλον παιδιον

καλον παιδιον

το παιδιον καλον

το παιδιον το καλον

καλον το παιδιον

παιδιον καλον

In the following examples, decide how the adjective ἀγαθος -η -ον is being used. Is it

(a) used with or without a definite article to describe a noun (e.g. a/the good prophet)?
(b) used without a definite article to imply the verb 'to be' (e.g. the prophet is good)?

(c) used with or without a definite article but always without a noun to stand in place of a noun (e.g. the good)?

Look first to see if it has a definite article immediately in front of it, then look to see if it goes with a noun or stands on its own. This should tell you what you need to know. Sometimes the position will help (the adjective is often near to the noun) or it may have the same ending. But your main clue is that the adjective has to have the same number, gender and case as the noun. The English translation from the NRSV is provided to help you. If all else fails, work it out from the English translation – normally there is only one option in the context:[4]

1 Romans 7: 12

So the law is holy, and the commandment is holy and just and **good**.

ὥστε ὁ μὲν νόμος ἅγιος καὶ ἡ ἐντολὴ ἁγία καὶ δικαία καὶ **ἀγαθή**.

2 1 Peter 2.18

* Slaves, accept the authority of your masters with all deference, not only the **good** and gentle ones but also the harsh ones.

Οἱ οἰκέται ὑποτασσόμενοι ἐν παντὶ φόβῳ τοῖς δεσπόταις, οὐ μόνον τοῖς **ἀγαθοῖς** καὶ ἐπιεικέσιν ἀλλὰ καὶ τοῖς σκολιοῖς.

3 Matthew 5.45

for he makes his sun rise on the evil and on the **good**, and sends rain on the righteous and on the unrighteous.

ὅτι τὸν ἥλιον αὐτοῦ ἀνατέλλει ἐπὶ πονηροὺς καὶ **ἀγαθοὺς** καὶ βρέχει ἐπὶ δικαίους καὶ ἀδίκους.

4 Matthew 7.17

In the same way, every **good** tree bears good fruit, but the bad tree bears bad fruit.

οὕτως πᾶν δένδρον **ἀγαθὸν** καρποὺς καλοὺς ποιεῖ, τὸ δὲ σαπρὸν δένδρον καρποὺς πονηροὺς ποιεῖ.

Note that two different words for 'good' are used here. Can you spot the other one?

THIS AND THAT, WHO AND WHICH

Demonstratives

The words 'this' and 'that' (sometimes called demonstratives) are important adjectives because they are used so often. Like other adjectives they can be used to describe a noun further (e.g. this book, that prophet), or on their own when they function as a noun, though we may need to add the words 'man', 'woman', 'thing', etc., in order to make sense of the Greek (e.g. this man, that thing).

Unlike other adjectives, 'this' and 'that' do not need to have a definite article in front of them. The noun they describe will have a definite article ('this' and 'that' indicate a definite, particular thing) but 'this' and 'that' will not. So if the Greek says something like 'this the prophet' or 'that the book' you need to supply the verb 'to be': 'this is the prophet', that is the book'.

The word 'that' (plural – 'those') is shown in Table 6.4. Do the endings in Table 6.4 look more like those for the definite article, or for adjectives?

The word 'this' (plural – 'these') is shown in Table 6.5. Again compare the endings in Table 6.5 to the definite article – do you notice any similarities?

Now look at these examples and translate the words in bold (they will either be 'this', 'these', 'that' or 'those'!) Check your answers in your English New Testament:

Table 6.4

Singular	Masculine	Feminine	Neuter
Nominative	ἐκεινος	ἐκεινη	ἐκεινο
Accusative	ἐκεινον	ἐκεινην	ἐκεινο
Genitive	ἐκεινου	ἐκεινης	ἐκεινου
Dative	ἐκεινῳ	ἐκεινῃ	ἐκεινῳ
Plural			
Nominative	ἐκεινοι	ἐκειναι	ἐκεινα
Accusative	ἐκεινους	ἐκεινας	ἐκεινα
Genitive	ἐκεινων	ἐκεινων	ἐκεινων
Dative	ἐκεινοις	ἐκειναις	ἐκεινοις

Table 6.5

Singular	Masculine	Feminine	Neuter
Nominative	οὑτος	αὑτη	τουτο
Accusative	τουτον	ταυτην	τουτο
Genitive	τουτου	ταυτης	τουτου
Dative	τουτῳ	ταυτῃ	τουτῳ
Plural			
Nominative	οὑτοι	αὑται	ταυτα
Accusative	τουτους	ταυτας	ταυτα
Genitive	τουτων	τουτων	τουτων
Dative	τουτοις	ταυταις	τουτοις

1 ἐὰν ὁ κύριος θελήσῃ καὶ ζήσομεν   καὶ
   If the Lord   wishes, (both) we-will-live (and also)

ποιήσομεν **τοῦτο** ἢ **ἐκεῖνο**.
   we-will-do   or
                                              (James 4.15)

2 Ἀλλὰ ἐν **ἐκείναις** ταῖς ἡμέραις μετὰ τὴν θλῖψιν **ἐκείνην**
   But in   days,   after   suffering

ὁ ἥλιος σκοτισθήσεται,
   the sun will-be-darkened
                                              (Mark 13.24)

3 **Οὗτος** ἐστιν ὁ μαθητὴς ὁ   μαρτυρῶν περὶ **τούτων** καὶ
            is the disciple who is-testifying to   and

ὁ   γράψας **ταῦτα**,
   (who) has-written
                                              (John 21.24)

4 καὶ λέγει αὐτοῖς· τίνος ἡ εἰκὼν **αὕτη** καὶ ἡ
   And he-said to-them, 'Whose (the) image   and (the)

ἐπιγραφή;
   inscription?
                                              (Matthew 22.20)

Note: the word τις (in this example it appears in the masculine
genitive singular, τινος) means 'who', 'what' or 'why'. In a normal sentence it means 'someone' or 'something'. Like πας it is
slightly irregular.

   If you are alert you will notice that αὕτη (example 4 above) is
very like αὐτη, the third person feminine pronoun. The differ-

ence between the two is a hard breathing for 'this' and a soft breathing for 'she'.

Look at the following sentences and decide which contain the feminine for 'this' and which contain the third person feminine pronoun (translated 'she', 'it' or 'they'). You can tell from the context as well as the Greek.[5]

1 **αὕτη** ἐστὶν ἡ μεγάλη καὶ πρώτη   ἐντολή.   δευτέρα
        is   the great and first commandment second

  δὲ ὁμοία **αὐτῇ**
  and like

(Matthew 22.38–39)

Can you spot two adjectives here and the noun that they go with?

2   ὁ   δὲ εἶπεν **αὐτῇ**· θυγάτηρ, ἡ πίστις σου
    the-one and he-said   daughter the faith of-you

  σέσωκεν σε·
  has-saved you

(Mark 5.34)

3 καὶ ἤνεγκεν τὴν κεφαλὴν αὐτοῦ ἐπὶ πίνακι καὶ ἔδωκεν
  and he-brought the head   of him on dish and he-gave

  αὐτὴν τῷ κορασίῳ, καὶ τὸ κοράσιον ἔδωκεν **αὐτὴν** τῇ
          to-the girl and the girl   gave   to-the

  μητρὶ **αὐτῆς**.
  mother

(Mark 6.28)

Note: Greek has the same problem as English here: who or what is being referred to with each αὐτη? You can only really tell from the context.

4 καὶ λέγει   αὐτοῖς· τίνος ἡ εἰκὼν **αὕτη** καὶ ἡ

and he says to-them whose the image   and the

ἐπιγραφή; λέγουσιν αὐτῷ· Καίσαρος.

inscription? they-said to-him   Caesar

(Matthew 22.20–21)

Make sure in all the above examples that you can put the
sentences into good English, and check your answers in your
English New Testament.

Relative Pronouns

We have looked so far at personal pronouns (I, me, my, etc.) and
reflexive pronouns (myself, etc.).

There is one remaining, very important, type of pronoun that
we need to look at here, called the **relative pronoun**. The relative
pronoun is used to replace a noun when two sentences have been
joined together, to avoid repeating the noun unnecessarily.

For example, 'You are calling the boy. The boy is running'
becomes 'You are calling the boy **who** is running'. Similarly, 'The
book is on the table. The book is red' becomes 'The book **which**
is on the table is red' or 'the book **that** is on the table is red'.

The forms of the relative pronoun are given in Table 6.6.
Again compare Table 6.6 with the definite article and see what
similarities and differences you can notice.

Now have a look at the following sentences and decide how
you should translate the relative pronoun (marked for you in
bold). When you have done this give a 'good' English translation
for the whole sentence and compare it with the same reading in
your English New Testament:[6]

1 ἰδόντες δὲ οἱ ἀρχιερεῖς καὶ οἱ γραμματεῖς τὰ θαυμάσια

seeing but the high-priests and the   scribes   the wonders

ἃ ἐποίησεν

he-did   (Matthew 21.15)

Table 6.6

Singular	Masculine	Feminine	Neuter	Meaning
Nominative	ὅς	ἥ	ὅ	who, that, which
Accusative	ὅν	ἥν	ὅ	whom, that, which
Genitive	οὗ	ἧς	οὗ	whose
Dative	ᾧ	ᾗ	ᾧ	to whom, to which
Plural				
Nominative	οἵ	αἵ	ἅ	who, that, which
Accusative	οὕς	ἅς	ἅ	whom, that, which
Genitive	ὧν	ὧν	ὧν	whose
Dative	οἷς	αἷς	οἷς	to whom, to which

2 καὶ Ἰούδαν Ἰσκαριώθ, **ὃς** καὶ παρέδωκεν αὐτόν.

  and Judas   Iscariot   and   betrayed him

(Mark 3.19)

Note: remember that και can mean 'also' as well as 'and'.

3 Εἶπεν δὲ πρὸς αὐτούς· οὗτοι οἱ λόγοι μου **οὓς** ἐλάλησα

  he-said and to   them these the words of-me   I-said

πρὸς ὑμᾶς

to   you

(Luke 24.44)

ADVERBS: A BRIEF NOTE

You will recall that an adjective is a way of describing something
or someone: it is associated with a noun or pronoun and gives
some extra information about it. An adverb does the same for an
action: it is associated with a verb (a 'doing' word) and tells you
something more about the way in which an action is taking
place. In English, adverbs often end in '-ly', for example:

She came silently into the room

He answered angrily

Suddenly, we felt ashamed

Adverbs have a similar simplicity in Greek, and compared to
adjectives are delightfully straightforward. Any given adverb
always looks exactly the same as it does in the dictionary. It can
appear anywhere in a sentence (though it is most often found at
the beginning, or near the verb) and can be easily recognized by
its -ως ending. Adverbs are relatively unusual: the following four
examples are the most common ones:

ἐσχάτως	finally, in the end
εὐθέως	immediately, at once
καλως	rightly, well
ὁμοιως or οὕτως	similarly, in the same way

LOOKING AT TRANSLATIONS

Remembering what we discussed in Chapter 5 about looking at
other translations, look at the following sentence with its accompanying translations:

οὕτως πᾶν δένδρον ἀγαθὸν καρποὺς καλοὺς ποιεῖ, τὸ δὲ

thus every tree   good   fruit   good makes, the but

σαπρὸν δένδρον καρποὺς πονηροὺς ποιεῖ. οὐ δύναται

rotten   tree   fruit   poor   makes not   able

δένδρον ἀγαθὸν καρποὺς πονηροὺς ποιεῖν   οὐδὲ   δένδρον

tree   good   fruit   poor   to-make and-not   tree

σαπρὸν καρποὺς καλοὺς ποιεῖν.

rotten   fruit   good to-make

(Matthew 7.17–18)

Use the knowledge you have gained in this chapter to work out how the adjectives ἀγαθὸν, καλοὺς, σαπρὸν and πονηροὺς fit into the sentence. Which adjective goes with which noun, and why?[7]

Note that the adjective καλος -η -ον is related to the adverb, καλως. A number of other adverbs are also formed by taking the stem of an adjective and adding -ως.

One of the reasons for getting to know Greek a little is so that you can begin to have a clearer idea of the depth of meaning of the Greek text. When translators translate the New Testament into English, they choose one possible meaning from a range of meanings for each Greek word. Sometimes this makes little difference (e.g. θεος is best translated 'God' wherever it appears) but other times this begins to make a lot of difference. Look up each of the four adjectives that we have already looked at – ἀγαθὸν, καλοὺς, σαπρὸν and πονηροὺς – in a dictionary or on a website and see what difference the alternative translations of the word make to the above passage.

Now look at the following translations:

In the same way, every good tree bears good fruit, but the bad tree bears bad fruit. A good tree cannot bear bad fruit, nor can a bad tree bear good fruit. (NRSV)

A healthy tree bears good fruit, but a poor tree bears bad fruit. A healthy tree cannot bear bad fruit, and a poor tree cannot bear good fruit. (GNB)

Even so every good tree bringeth forth good fruit; but a corrupt tree bringeth forth evil fruit. A good tree cannot bring forth evil fruit, neither can a corrupt tree bring forth good fruit. (KJV)

Go through each translation carefully and ask:

- What words have been missed out – how important is this?
- What do you think about the choice of translations of the adjectives in this passage?
- Which one do you prefer and why?
- Do you want to alter any part of your preferred translation in the light of what the Greek says?

Use your knowledge of the possible translations of the adjectives to help you answer the questions.

REVIEW OF LEARNING

In this chapter we have looked at:

- use of word order and the definite article with adjectives;
- different ways of using adjectives;
- demonstratives and relative pronouns;
- adverbs.

Notes

1 The articles you should have circled are: (1) ἡ (twice), (2) ὁ (once), (3) την (once).

2 (1) The NRSV reads: 'do not imitate **what is** evil but imitate **what is** good'. (2) The NRSV does not add anything – 'the good' refers to the fish mentioned in the previous verse.

3 το καλον παιδιον – the good child
καλον παιδιον – a good child
το παιδιον καλον – the child is good
το παιδιον το καλον – the good child
καλον το παιδιον – the child is good
παιδιον καλον – a good child

4 (1) Option (b): the commandment is holy and just and good;
(2) Option (c): standing in place of the noun, literally 'the good ones';
(3) Option (c) again;
(4) Option (a).

5 (1) This . . . it, the two adjectives are μεγαλη and πρωτη and the noun that they go with is ἐντολη; (2) to her ; (3) it, it, her; (4) this.

6 (1) that or which (neut pl acc), (2) who (msc sg nom), (3) that or which (msc pl acc).

7 ἀγαθὸν describes the noun δένδρον; they are both neuter singular accusative (but their endings are the same as those for masculine singular accusative). καλοὺς describes the noun καρπους; they are both masculine plural accusative. σαπρὸν describes the noun δένδρον; they are both neuter singular accusative (but their endings are the same as those for masculine singular accusative). πονηροὺς describes the noun καρποὺς; they are both masculine plural accusative.

7

Simple Verbs

In this chapter we begin to look at verbs – the words that describe the *action* in a sentence. All the verbs we will look at in this chapter describe action as it is happening 'now' (the present tense) and focus attention on the person doing the action (they are 'active'). They are therefore sometimes referred to as **present, active** verbs. Where they differ is in a curious Greek property called their 'mood', which refers to the way in which the verb describes the action. The first and most straightforward ones are sometimes called **indicatives**, because they describe a definite action; we will then go on to look at the **subjunctive** (which expresses uncertainty); the **imperative** (which turns the verb into a command); and the **infinitive** (which makes a general statement).

-ω VERBS

The first sort of verb we will look at is called in some grammars and commentaries the **present indicative active**. They can be simply translated as, for example, 'I am doing', 'you are doing', etc.

As with nouns, verbs in Greek carry more information than their English equivalents. In English we need to have pronouns (or nouns) alongside verbs so that we can tell who, or what, is doing the action: Greek verbs may sometimes have pronouns with them to emphasize who is performing the action, but normally they do not. Instead, in Greek the same job is done by the verb ending. The stem tells you what the verb means, and the ending tells you who is doing the action (I, you, he, she, it, we, you, they).

Like nouns, then, verbs in Greek have a stem (which does not change) and an ending (which changes according to who is the subject of the action, or what sort of verb we are looking at). We need to be able to recognize what counts as the stem and what counts as an ending. Then we need to identify different endings so that we can work out who is doing what in a sentence.

The most straightforward examples are sometimes referred to as -ω verbs because the form you will see in the dictionary consists of the stem for the present tense and the ending -ω. This is the **first person singular present indicative active** form, for example, λεγω, meaning 'I speak', or ἀποστελλω, meaning 'I send' etc.

Look at the following sentences, all containing the Greek verb λεγω:

1 ἐγὼ δὲ λέγω ὑμῖν

  I   but I-say to-you

(Matthew 5.22)

2 Τοῦτο γὰρ ὑμῖν λέγομεν ἐν λόγῳ κυρίου

  this   for to-you we-say in word of-Lord

(1 Thessalonians 4.15)

3 λέγετε   ὅτι δοῦλοι ἀχρεῖοι ἐσμεν,

  you (plural)-say that slaves useless we-are

(Luke 17.10)

4 οὐκ οἶδα   τί λέγεις

  not I-know what you (singular)-say

(Matthew 26.70)

5 καὶ λέγουσιν αὐτῷ οἱ μαθηταί·

and they-say to-him the disciples

(Matthew 15.33)

6 καὶ λέγει αὐτῷ ὁ Ἰησοῦς

and he-says to-him the Jesus

(Matthew 8.4)

> In the last two examples, 'says' is in the present tense, but it is
> translated in the NRSV as if it were in the past tense. This is
> termed the **historical present**. In English, when people are
> speaking colloquially, they might slip into the present tense
> when recounting a story that happened in the past. For
> example, 'I was walking down the street and I see an old
> lady and she says to me . . .' This happens often in Greek,
> especially in the Gospels. You will find that quite often the
> present tense is used even though the action described is in
> the past. English translations iron out these wrinkles by trans-
> lating the verb in the past tense to make it all make more
> sense.

In each of the sentences above:

- note which bit of the word is the stem (i.e. the bit that never changes);
- then for each word take away the stem and you will be left with the ending;
- then work out what each form of the word means (e.g. λεγω means 'I say', what does λεγεις mean?).

Write the endings and the meanings in Table 7.1.[1]

Table 7.1

Form of Word	Meaning		Ending
λεγω	I say	first person singular	-ω
λεγεις		second person singular	
λεγει		third person singular	
λεγομεν		first person plural	
λεγετε		second person plural	
λεγουσι(ν)		third person plural	

Note: the third person plural sometimes appears with a ν and sometimes without one, so the ν is given in brackets.

The endings that you have just identified are the endings you will find on most verbs. In Table 7.2, practise the same skills on some different verb-stems:

• separate the stem and the ending of the word;

• work out what pronoun needs to be given in English to reflect its ending (e.g. I see, you see, etc.);

• then look up the verb in its first person singular form (e.g. βλεπω, λεγω) using a website or dictionary so that you can see what it means.[2]

Table 7.2

Greek word	Stem	Meaning of ending (I, you, he/she/it, we, you, they)	Meaning of the stem
βλεπεις	βλεπ	you (sg)	see
γινωσκετε			
λυει			
πιστευω			
πεμπει			
γραφομεν			
ἀκουετε			
κρινουσιν			
λαμβανεις			

Further Practice with -ω Verbs

Look at the following Greek sentences and indicate which of the translations is correct:[3]

ι τοῦτο οὖν ποίησον ὅ σοι λέγομεν

   this therefore do what you say

(Acts 21.23)

Possible translations:

(a) Therefore do this thing that I am saying to you.

(b) Therefore do this thing that you are saying.

(c) Therefore do this thing that we are saying to you.

2 καὶ τὴν μαρτυρίαν αὐτοῦ οὐδεὶς λαμβάνει
  and the   witness   he   no-one receive

(John 3.32)

Possible translations:

(a) And you receive no one's witness.
(b) And no one receives his witness.
(c) And they receive his witness.

3 Τί δὲ βλέπεις τὸ κάρφος τὸ   ἐν τῷ ὀφθαλμῷ τοῦ
   why but see   the stalk the-one in the   eye   the

ἀδελφοῦ σοῦ
brother you

(Matthew 7.3)

Possible translations:

(a) Why does he see the stalk in your brother's eye?
(b) Why do we see the stalk in our brother's eye?
(c) Why do you see the stalk in your brother's eye?

4   αὐτὰ   τὰ ἔργα ἃ   ποιῶ μαρτυρεῖ περὶ ἐμοῦ
    themselves the works which I-do bear-witness about me

(John 5.36)

Possible translations:

(a) He bears witness about me that I do the same works.
(b) The same works which I do bear witness about me.
(c) I bear witness about the works that I do.

Note: one peculiarity of Greek is that neuter plural nouns sometimes (but not always!) take on verbs in the singular. In this case, the noun, τὰ ἔργα (the works) is plural but the verb, μαρτυρεῖ (it bears witness) is singular.

CONTRACTED VERBS

The verbs that we have looked at so far have a stem that either ends in a consonant (e.g. λεγω where the stem is λεγ) or a stem that ends in a vowel that never changes (e.g. λυω where the stem is λυ).

Some verbs have stems that end in α, ο or ε (e.g. ἐρωταω, σταυροω and ποιεω). It is quite obvious that these are going to cause problems. If you try to simply remove the -ω and add other verb endings, they not only look odd, but they are difficult to pronounce. For example, ἐρωταεις, σταυροουσιν and ποιεει are wrong.

When you try changing the endings of these verbs, there are simply too many vowels in the words. What happens instead is that the vowels contract (hence their name contracted verbs) and one vowel replaces two. There are certain rules that govern this but you don't need to know them now because, by definition, in the Greek text that you have in front of you the contraction has already taken place.

You can tell it has happened by:

- a slightly strange ending for the verb;

- a circumflex accent ^ over the vowel that has contracted. This is helpful, but only applies in the present tense.

So the vowels between the stem and the ending in the three examples above contract to give the following:

ἐρωτᾷς

σταυροῦσιν

ποιεῖ

Look at the following sentences and circle the verbs that have been contracted (don't forget the give away circumflex). Also see if you can turn the interlinear translations of the verses into good English:[4]

1 Οὐαὶ ὑμῖν τοῖς Φαρισαίοις, ὅτι   ἀγαπᾶτε τὴν

  Woe to-you   Pharisees because you-love the

  πρωτοκαθεδρίαν ἐν ταῖς συναγωγαῖς

    best-seats   in   the   synagogues

                                        (Luke 11.43)

2 τί   ποιεῖτε κλαίοντες καὶ συνθρύπτοντες μου τὴν καρδίαν;

  what you-doing weeping and   crushing   me the   heart

                                        (Acts 21.13)

3 τί   με ἐρωτᾷς περὶ τοῦ ἀγαθοῦ;

  why me you-ask about the   good?

                                        (Matthew 19.17)

THE VERB 'TO BE' AND OTHERS LIKE IT

εἰμι (I am)

In this and in previous chapters you may have noticed the
frequent use of the verb 'to be'. If you have, you may be feeling
confused since the verb 'to be' looks nothing like the verbs we
have just been looking at.

This is because it belongs to a small group of verbs in Greek
which do not have -ω at the end of the first person singular
present form (like λεγω and βλεπω) but have -μι instead. This
characteristic means that they are often called -μι verbs (for
obvious reasons!). The first person singular present of 'to be' is
εἰμι (I am).

Just to make things even more difficult, εἰμι is what we call an
irregular verb. This means that it doesn't even properly obey
the rules for -μι verbs. For this reason you will probably come to

recognize this verb by its context in the sentence (and your interlinear!) rather than by detailed knowledge of its endings, but
if you want to see the full form of εἰμι you will find it in the
appendix (Table A.12). For now, however, look at the following
sentences and notice the different forms of εἰμι – you may find
you recognize some of them already:

1 Ἐγώ εἰμι ὁ   ποιμὴν   ὁ καλὸς

   I   I-am the shepherd the good

(John 10.14)

2 εἰ υἱὸς   εἶ   τοῦ θεοῦ,

   If son you-are of-the God

(Luke 4.3)

Notice that, in the last example, there is another little word
very similar to εἶ, 'you are'; it is εἰ, meaning 'if'. The only way
to tell the two words apart is by the circumflex accent over ι
in the verb 'you are'. This is one of those occasions when
accents are hugely important.

---

3 ὁμοία ἐστὶν ἡ βασιλεία τῶν   οὐρανῶν κόκκῳ σινάπεως,

   like   it-is the kingdom of-the heavens a grain mustard

(Matthew 13.31)

4 ἐγὼ καὶ ὁ πατὴρ ἕν ἐσμεν.

   I   and the father one we-are

(John 10.30)

Note the word ἕν, meaning 'one'. It looks like the word ἐν (in),
but has a rough breathing instead of a smooth breathing.

5 ὑμεῖς ἐστε τὸ ἅλας τῆς γῆς·

   you   you-are the salt of-the earth

(Matthew 5.13)

6 τίς ἐστιν ἡ μήτηρ μου καὶ τίνες εἰσὶν οἱ ἀδελφοί μου;

   who is   the mother of-me and who   are the brothers of-me?

(Matthew 12.48)

You may find it helpful to fill in Table 7.3 as you did for λεγω in Table 7.1.[5]

Table 7.3

Form of Word	Meaning	
εἰμι		first person singular
εἶ		second person singular
ἐστι(ν)		third person singular
ἐσμεν		first person plural
ἐστε		second person plural
εἰσι(ν)		third person plural

One of the slightly confusing things about the verb 'to be' is that it never has an object. You will only ever find subjects around the verb 'to be'. This is because the verb 'to be' is not an action word – it never 'does' anything to anyone or anything else. Instead it acts like an 'equals' (=) sign. For example:

οὗτος   ἐστιν ὁ   υἱός μου   ὁ   ἀγαπητός

this (person) is   the son of-me the   beloved

(Matthew 3.17)

This could also be written: 'this person = my beloved son' or 'my beloved son = this person'. The two are exactly parallel statements and can be written in either order without changing the meaning.

Other -μι Verbs

You have encountered the bad news about -μι verbs already: they are different from -ω verbs. To make things more confusing, there are a few common -μι verbs (like ἀπολλυμι below) that sometimes have the endings for -ω verbs in New Testament Greek. This is because people who didn't speak the language very well often didn't understand -μι endings. Then as now, they tended to leave people confused!

Because these endings are quite complex, it is not necessary to learn them here. (There is a chart of διδωμι, 'to give', the commonest of these verbs, in the appendix (Table A.13) if you want to look at it.) You should simply be aware that you will sometimes come across a type of verb that looks different from the ones you are used to. Be prepared to work out what they mean by looking at their context, an interlinear Bible, or a website. The good news is that there aren't very many of them!

The following sentences will give you practice in working out the meaning of the -μι verb from the context. For each one, try and work out what person (first, second or third) and what number (singular or plural) you think the verb is. Don't try to work this out from its *ending*, but instead have a guess at it from the *context*. In each case, the -μι verb is in bold:

1 ἀλλ' ὁ πατήρ μου **δίδωσιν** ὑμῖν τὸν ἄρτον ἐκ τοῦ οὐρανοῦ
but the father of-me gives to-you the bread from the heaven

τὸν ἀληθινόν·
the true

(John 6.32)

2 Οὐδεὶς δὲ λύχνον ἅψας καλύπτει αὐτὸν σκεύει ἢ
No-one lamp lighting hides it in-a-container or

ὑποκάτω κλίνης **τίθησιν**, ἀλλ' ἐπὶ λυχνίας **τίθησιν**,
under bed places but upon lampstand places

(Luke 8.16)

3 ὁ φιλῶν τὴν ψυχὴν αὐτοῦ **ἀπολλύει** αὐτήν,
the-one loving the soul of-him loses it

(John 12.25)

Note: this is an example of a -μι verb that uses some endings like
-ω verbs. Compare the verb ending in the example with the third
person singular ending for λεγω and you will see that it is the
same!

If you have interpreted the context correctly, you will have
noticed that all these verbs are third person singular. You will
find these verbs most often in this form (remember that they are
not that common) and may begin to recognize the ending after a
while.

CHANGES OF MOOD: SUBJUNCTIVES, IMPERATIVES AND INFINITIVES

The verbs that we have looked at so far this chapter are described as being in the indicative mood. Indicatives are the ordinary form of the verb (e.g. I go, I sit, I stand, etc.). In them, the subject does the verb: indicatives describe a definite action.

As well as the indicative, there are other moods called the subjunctive, imperative and infinitive. What connects them is that the action isn't simply being described, but is being talked about in the abstract. Briefly, subjunctives talk about what might happen, imperatives about what must happen, and infinitives about 'happening' in general! This will become clearer as we look at each in more detail.

Subjunctives

Whereas indicatives indicate definite action (I sit, I go, etc.), subjunctives indicate indefinite action (I might sit, if I were to go, etc.). Their endings differ from normal indicative endings by a lengthening of the final vowel (where this is possible) as shown in Table 7.4.

Table 7.4

	Present Subjunctive Active
first person singular	λεγω
second person singular	λεγῃς
third person singular	λεγῃ
first person plural	λεγωμεν
second person plural	λεγητε
third person plural	λεγωσι(ν)

You will notice that λεγω is no different as its vowel cannot get any longer, but the vowels of the other forms become a long version of what they were before, e.g. λυεις becomes λυῃς because η is the longer version of ε and because ι cannot go alongside η it drops below it.

Have a look at some of the uses of the subjunctive below and notice what difference they make to the sense of the sentence. Verbs in the subjunctive are in bold:

1 ἐὰν οὖν   **προσφέρῃς**   τὸ δῶρόν σου ἐπὶ τὸ

   if therefore you-were-to-bring the gift of-you to   the

θυσιαστήριον κἀκεῖ   **μνησθῇς**   ὅτι ὁ ἀδελφός

   altar   and-there you-were-to-remember that the brother

σου ἔχει   τι   κατὰ σοῦ,

   of-you has something against you

                            (Matthew 5.23)

This is a hypothetical situation. It doesn't refer to an actual event but to something that might happen.

2 ὃς γὰρ ἐὰν   **θέλῃ**   τὴν ψυχὴν αὐτοῦ σῶσαι ἀπολέσει

   who for ever might-want the   soul of-him to-save he-will-lose

αὐτήν· ὃς δ᾽ ἂν **ἀπολέσῃ** τὴν ψυχὴν αὐτοῦ   ἕνεκεν

   it   who but ever might-lose the   soul of-him for-the-sake

ἐμοῦ εὑρήσει αὐτήν.

   of-me will-find   it

                            (Matthew 16.25)

This famous passage from Matthew reminds us what will happen to two hypothetical types of people: those who seek to save their souls and those who lose them.

3 Ὅταν   δὲ   **διώκωσιν** ὑμᾶς ἐν τῇ πόλει ταύτῃ,

whenever but they-might-pursue you in the city   this

φεύγετε εἰς τὴν ἑτέραν

flee   into the other

(Matthew 10.23)

Again, a hypothetical situation: Jesus is telling the disciples what to do in response to something that might happen.

As well as these basic meanings of the subjunctive, it can also be used with the little word 'ἵνα', which means 'so that'. For example:

ἵνα   δὲ   **εἰδῆτε**   ὅτι ἐξουσίαν ἔχει ὁ υἱὸς

so-that but you-might-see that   authority has the son

τοῦ ἀνθρώπου

of-the man

(Matthew 9.6)

Practice with Subjunctives

In the following sentences, the verbs in bold are subjunctives. From the basic meanings of the words provided, work out what the sentence should mean if translated in the subjunctive (then check your English Bibles and see if they reflect this!).

You will notice that each of these sentences uses a small word ending in αν (ἐάν, ἂν and ὅταν). These little words often (though not always) mark the presence of a subjunctive and are best translated as 'ever' (e.g. if ever, whenever, etc.):

1 καὶ ἐὰν **ἀγαθοποιῆτε** τοὺς ἀγαθοποιοῦντας ὑμᾶς,

and if   do-good-to those   doing-good-to you,

ποία   ὑμῖν χάρις ἐστίν;

of-what-sort to-you grace   is-it

(Luke 6.33)

2 καὶ ἐάν   τις ὑμᾶς **ἐρωτᾷ·** διὰ   τί   λύετε;

and if someone you   ask because-of what are-you-untying

οὕτως ἐρεῖτε· ὅτι ὁ κύριος αὐτοῦ χρείαν ἔχει.

so   you-say that the Lord   of-it need   has

(Luke 19.31)

Imperatives

Both indicatives and subjunctives are descriptive forms of the
verb. They describe action, either definitely or indefinitely.
Imperatives do not describe action, but command it – 'do this',
'sit there'. They can be in the singular or plural. They are most
commonly found in the second person ('you do this') but can also
be found in the third person ('let him or her do this', 'let them do
this').

Their endings are listed in Table 7.5.

Table 7.5

	Present Imperative Active
second person singular	λεγε
third person singular	λεγετω
second person plural	λεγετε
third person plural	λεγετωσαν

Note: it is very easy to confuse the second person plural imperative ending with the second person plural indicative ending
(see Table 7.1). The only thing you can do in such instances is
to look at the context and decide from that what the word
means.

Practice with Imperatives

Have a look at the following sentences. The verbs in bold are imperatives. From the basic meanings of the words provided work out what the sentences mean. Check your answers with an English New Testament:

1 προσελθὼν   δὲ   ὁ χιλίαρχος εἶπεν αὐτῷ· **λέγε** μοι, σὺ

 approaching but the chiliarch   said   he   say me you

ʽΡωμαῖος   εἶ;

 Roman you-are

(Acts 22.27)

Note: a chiliarch is a commander of a thousand soldiers, as opposed to a centurion who is the commander of a hundred.

2 τότε   οἱ   ἐν τῇ Ἰουδαίᾳ **φευγέτωσαν** εἰς τὰ   ὄρη,

 then the-ones in the Judea   flee   into the mountains

(Matthew 24.16)

3 καὶ ἔλεγεν· ὃς ἔχει ὦτα ἀκούειν **ἀκουέτω**.

 and he-said who has ears to-hear   hear

(Mark 4.9)

Infinitives

The good news about the infinitive is that, unlike the other types of verbs we have looked at in this chapter, its ending does not change. The basic form of the infinitive of -ω type verbs looks like this: λέγειν.

Infinitives have a simple and a complex use. In this chapter we will look just at their simple use (for their more complex use see Chapter 10). The simple use of an infinitive is always translated as 'to . . .' (e.g. to speak, to sit, to walk, etc.). Consequently, when used like this, the infinitive is always dependent upon another verb such as 'I am about to go', 'I am able to eat'. Although infinitives can be found after a range of different verbs, there are certain verbs which we normally expect to have an infinitive after them, in both Greek and English:

ἄρχομαι	I am beginning to . . .
δει	it is necessary to . . .
δυναμαι	I am able to . . .
ἐξεστιν	it is lawful/permitted to . . .
μελλω	I am about / intend to . . .

Knowing this, look at the following sentences and see if you can work out what the phrases in bold mean (you will be given enough words to help you but the verbs mentioned in the list above will not be translated again here) and then from that, see if you can work out what the whole sentence means. Check your answers with an English New Testament:

1 ἰδοὺ   οἱ μαθηταί σου ποιοῦσιν ὃ οὐκ **ἔξεστιν ποιεῖν** ἐν

behold the disciples you   do   what not   do   in

σαββάτῳ

sabbath

(Matthew 12.2)

2 **δύνασθε πιεῖν** τὸ ποτήριον ὃ ἐγὼ **μέλλω πίνειν**;

you-are-able drink the   cup which I   drink

(Matthew 20.22)

Note: don't forget the importance of the ; at the end of the sentence.

3 εἴσελθε εἰς τὴν πόλιν καὶ λαληθήσεταί σοι ὅ τί

go-into into the   city and it-will-be-told you what

σε δεῖ ποιεῖν.

you   do

(Acts 9.6)

MORE ON NEGATIVES

The Use of οὐ and μη

In Chapter 2 you encountered the negatives οὐ, οὐκ, οὐχ and μη. At the time, you may have wondered why there were two different ways of saying 'no' (those from the οὐ group and μη). The answer is that the choice of negative depends on the type of verb that is used.

- οὐ is used to negate a verb in the indicative.

- μη is used to negate everything else (including subjunctives, imperatives, infinitives and participles).

Compare for example:

1 οὐ λέγω σοι ἕως ἑπτάκις ἀλλὰ ἕως ἑβδομηκοντάκις

not I-say to-you until seven-times but until seventy-times

ἑπτά.

seven

(Matthew 18.22)

Note: λέγω is here in the indicative form.

2 ὃ   οὖν ὁ θεὸς   συνέζευξεν   ἄνθρωπος μὴ

what therefore the God has-yoked-together humankind not

χωριζέτω

let-divide

(Matthew 19.6)

Note: χωριζέτω is in the imperative here.

Negatives in Questions

The only exception to the above rule is where οὐ and μη are used in questions. Here they have a special and unusual use.

- when a question begins with οὐ, the questioner expects the answer 'yes'. For example, οὐ βλέπετε ταῦτα πάντα; (Matthew 24.2) means 'Do you see all these things?' The expected answer is 'yes'.

- When a question begins with μη, the questioner expects the answer 'no'. For example, μὴ πάντες ἀπόστολοι; (1 Corinthians 12.29) means 'Are all apostles?' The expected answer is 'no'.

Compound Negatives

In addition to the simple negatives, οὐ and μη, it is possible to make longer words with negative meaning, as it is in English. In English, 'no' can be tacked onto 'one' to become 'no-one' and onto 'thing' to be 'nothing' etc.; this can also happen in Greek. Here are the commonest examples:

οὐδε/μηδε	and not
οὐδε . . . οὐδε . . ./μηδε . . . μηδε . . .	neither . . . nor
οὐδεποτε/μηδεποτε	never
οὐδεπω/μηδεπω	not yet

οὐκετι/μηκετι	no longer
οὐπω/μηπω	not yet
οὐδεις/μηδεις	no-one/nothing

Note: οὐδεις and μηδεις have a stem and an ending. The stems are οὐδ- and μηδ- respectively. The endings are complex; it is not necessary to learn them now, but you will see one in the example that follows in *Double Negatives*. See if you can spot it.[6]

It is also worth noticing that ἱνα μη, 'so that not', is best translated into English as 'lest'.

Double Negatives

In English, two negatives form a positive statement. For example, 'I am not uneducated' means 'I am educated'. But in Greek a second negative just reinforces the first one: 'I am not uneducated' means 'I am not, definitely not, educated!' Here is an example that includes a double negative. Decide which is the best translation:[7]

ὑμεῖς   κατὰ   τὴν σάρκα κρίνετε, ἐγὼ οὐ κρίνω οὐδένα.

you according-to the flesh   judge   I   not judge no-one

(John 8.15)

Possible translations:

(a) You judge according to the flesh, I do not judge anyone.

(b) They judge you according to the flesh, I do not judge anyone.

(c) You judge according to the flesh, I judge everyone.

LOOKING AT TRANSLATIONS

Look at the following well-known passage. The major words have been translated for you but the small words like 'and', 'but', 'so that' and 'the' have been missed out so you will need to try and work out or remember what they mean:

John 3.16–17

οὕτως γὰρ ἠγάπησεν ὁ θεὸς τὸν κόσμον, ὥστε τὸν υἱὸν τὸν

thus   loved   God   world therefore   son

μονογενη ἔδωκεν, ἵνα πᾶς ὁ πιστεύων εἰς αὐτὸν μὴ

only-begotten gave   every   believing   in   him

ἀπόληται   ἀλλ᾽ ἔχῃ   ζωὴν αἰώνιον. οὐ γὰρ

might-be-destroyed   might-have life   eternal

ἀπέστειλεν ὁ θεὸς τὸν υἱὸν εἰς τὸν κόσμον ἵνα   κρίνῃ

sent   God   son into   world   might-judge

τὸν κόσμον, ἀλλ᾽ ἵνα   σωθῇ   ὁ κόσμος   δι᾽ αὐτοῦ.

world   might-be-saved   world through him

Look up the following words to gain a greater insight into the full range of their meaning:

μονογενῆ   πιστεύων   ἀπόληται   κρίνῃ

(**Hint:** use the dictionary on the *Crosswalk* site, http://bible. crosswalk.com/Lexicons/NewTestamentGreek/ to help you find the stems and the meanings of the words.)

Then have a look at the three translations of these verses given below and ask yourself the following questions:

- Do any of them miss out or add in words – how legitimate do you think this is?

- Which one do you like the best and why?

- Has any one translation captured the meaning of the Greek better than another – note particularly the way they have translated the subjunctive, of which there are four (ἀπόληται, ἔχῃ, κρίνῃ and σωθῇ). Which one works best in your opinion?

For God so loved the world that He gave His only begotten Son, that whoever believes in Him should not perish but have everlasting life. For God did not send His Son into the world to condemn the world, but that the world through Him might be saved. (NKJV)

For God so loved the world that he gave his one and only Son, that whoever believes in him shall not perish but have eternal life. For God did not send his Son into the world to condemn the world, but to save the world through him. (NIV)

For God so loved the world that he gave his only Son, so that everyone who believes in him will not perish but have eternal life. God did not send his Son into the world to condemn it, but to save it. (NLB)

REVIEW OF LEARNING

In this chapter we have looked at:

- -ω and -μι verbs in the present indicative;

- the subjunctive, imperative and infinitive types of verb;

- more on negatives.

Notes

1 Your chart should look like this:

Form of Word	Meaning		Ending
λεγω	I say	first person singular	-ω
λεγεις	you (sg) say	second person singular	-εις
λεγει	she/he/it says	third person singular	-ει
λεγομεν	we say	first person plural	-ομεν
λεγετε	you (pl) say	second person plural	-ετε
λεγουσι(ν)	they say	third person plural	-ουσι(ν)

2 Your chart should look like this:

Greek word	Stem	Meaning of ending (I, you, he/she/it, we, you, they)	Meaning of the stem
βλεπεις	βλεπ	you (sg)	see
γινωσκετε	γινωσκ	you (pl)	know
λυει	λυ	she/he/it	looses
πιστευω	πιστευ	I	believe
πεμπει	πεμπ	she/he/it	sends
γραφομεν	γραφ	we	write
ἀκουετε	ἀκου	you (pl)	hear
κρινουσιν	κριν	they	judge
λαμβανεις	λαμβαν	you (sg)	take

3 (1) c, (2) b, (3) c, (4) b.

4 The contracted verbs are: (1) ἀγαπᾶτε, (2) ποιεῖτε, (3) ἐρωτᾷς.

5 Your table should look like this:

Form of Word	Meaning	
εἰμι	I am	first person singular
εἶ	you (sg) are	second person singular
ἐστι(ν)	she/he/it is	third person singular
ἐσμεν	we are	first person plural
ἐστε	you (pl) are	second person plural
εἰσι(ν)	they are	third person plural

6 οὐδένα

7 (b)

8

Tenses

In Chapter 7, we saw how the endings of a verb tell you the person and number of those doing the action (i.e. whether it's performed by I, you, he/she/it, we, you or they). We also looked at the different moods: the definite (indicative), indefinite (subjunctive), command (imperative) and abstract (some uses of the infinitive) types. All the verbs we looked at there were in the present tense (i.e. the action is happening now) because in most ways this is the simplest place to start.

However, a whole range of additional shades of meaning in verbs can be achieved by changing the tense. Greek has quite a number of these and is often precise in its use of them. This means that our understanding of the New Testament will be much richer when we understand what tenses a writer is using, and why. In this chapter we will be looking at what each of the commonest tenses mean and how to begin to recognize them.

STEMS AND ENDINGS, ADDITIONS AND INSERTS

In the present tense the verb, as we have seen, is formed by adding endings onto a basic stem, for example, λεγ (the stem) has ω, εις, ει, ομεν, ετε, ουσιν (the endings) added to it to form the verb. However, when the tense of a verb changes in Greek, other changes to the verb may also be made:

- a letter, or letters, may be added to the beginning of the stem;
- an extra letter may be inserted between the stem and the ending;

- a distinctive set of endings are added in each tense;
- even the stem itself may change.

Because there are so many potential changes, it is very important to be able to recognize a basic stem, where possible, as this
gives you all sorts of clues about what has been added to the verb
in order to reach the form that it has. To sum up, a word may be
changed in four different ways as it moves from one tense to
another:

Addition	Stem	Insert	Ending

For example, the first person singular perfect indicative active
of πιστευω is πεπιστευκα, 'I have believed'. It breaks down as
follows:

Addition	Stem	Insert	Ending
πε	πιστευ	κ	α

Consequently when you are trying to recognize a verb in a
tense other than the present, you need to look for four things: the
stem, any additions to the stem, any insert and the endings.
Between them, they will tell you what tense the verb is.

In Chapter 7 we used the verb λεγω to see how changes to the
verb take place because it is used so often in the New Testament
that it helps to become familiar with it. However, λεγω does
something rather odd in its other tenses, so instead of using
it here we will now change the verb to πιστευω 'I believe' to
illustrate the changes that take place.

In this chapter you will be shown lots of tables of verbs. Do
not try to memorize them, and attempt not to be overawed by
them. They are here to show you basic patterns of changes in the
tenses – look for these and don't worry too much about the
specific endings that you will see.

CHANGES BETWEEN THE STEM AND THE ENDING: THE FUTURE TENSE

The future tense in Greek, as in English, refers quite simply to events that will take place in the future.

The form of the future tense is very like the form of the present tense with just one exception. Look at Table 8.1 and see if you can work out what it is.

Table 8.1

Person	Present Indicative Active	Future Indicative Active
1st singular	πιστευω	πιστευσω
2nd singular	πιστευεις	πιστευσεις
3rd singular	πιστευει	πιστευσει
1st plural	πιστευομεν	πιστευσομεν
2nd plural	πιστευετε	πιστευσετε
3rd plural	πιστευουσι(ν)	πιστευσουσι(ν)

You probably noticed that the future tense has an extra σ in the middle of it. It is formed by inserting a σ between the stem and the ending. The endings are the same as for the present tense. We can write it out like this:

Addition	Stem	Insert	Ending
-	**πιστευ**	σ	ω

Look at the verbs in Table 8.2 and work out what their stem is, what their tense is (future or present) and whether they are first, second or third person singular or plural. Finally, work out what they mean with the help of a dictionary or website. The first one has been done for you.[1]

Table 8.2

verb	basic stem	tense	person	meaning
ἀκουσεις	ἀκου-	future	2nd sing	you will hear
θεραπευετε				
βασιλευσει				
θεραπευσω				
ἀκουομεν				
βασιλευουσιν				

You will notice that you have two examples of each verb, one in the present tense and one in the future. This is to help you to identify the difference between the present and future form of each verb.

Remember: if you look up the verb in a dictionary or website it will appear in the first person singular present indicative active form.

Difficulties with the Formation of the Future Tense

If you look at the stems of the words you found above, you will notice that they all end with the letter υ. This is because σ can be added to these types of words very simply.

There are other letters that cause more problems when you add σ to them. These are worth spending a bit of time understanding.

- if you add σ to κ, γ, or χ, the resulting sounds are 'ks', 'gs', 'chs' – in Greek there is a letter so like this sound (ξ) that it is used instead. For example, διωκω, in the future tense, becomes διωξω.

- if you add σ to π, β or φ then the letter ψ is produced. For example, γραφω becomes γραψω.

- if you add σ to τ, δ, θ or ζ they become impossible to pronounce (try saying them and you'll see the problem) so the letter τ, δ, θ or ζ drops out and is replaced by σ. For example, βαπτιζω becomes βαπτισω.

- if you add σ to the vowels α, ε or ο, they become the nearest long vowel, so ε becomes η, ο becomes ω and α, because it does not have its own long vowel, borrows η. For example, ἀγαπαω becomes ἀγαπησω and φανεροω becomes φανερωσω.

- the most complex of all are verbs that end in λ, μ, ν or ρ. With these verbs neither the original letter changes nor the σ appears. Instead you find a diphthong before the ending. For example, μενομεν in the present becomes μενουμεν in the future.

This all appears to be very complicated but in practice is simpler than you might expect. If you were looking up the verb βαπτισω in the dictionary you wouldn't find it but if you looked around a bit you would find βαπτιζω and hence the meaning of the word.

Also, as you are most likely to be reading an interlinear Bible or using a website, you should, in most cases, have sufficient help in finding the meaning of the word. It is, however, worth being aware of why the verbs change as they do so that you know why they look as they do.

CHANGES AT THE BEGINNING OF THE STEM: THE IMPERFECT TENSE

The imperfect tense, as in English, refers to an action in the past which has begun but which may or may not have finished.

To make the imperfect tense, Greek adds an ἐ at the beginning of the stem and a different set of endings. Glance at Table 8.3 to see a typical example of the imperfect tense.

Table 8.3

Person	Imperfect Indicative Active
1st singular	ἐπιστευον
2nd singular	ἐπιστευες
3rd singular	ἐπιστευε(ν)
1st plural	ἐπιστευομεν
2nd plural	ἐπιστευετε
3rd plural	ἐπιστευον

If you remember that the stem is πιστευ here you will see that nothing has been inserted between the stem and the *endings*. However, ἐ has been added to the *beginning*:

Addition	Stem	Insert	Ending
ἐ	πιστευ	-	ον

Difficulties with the Formation of the Imperfect Tense

The problems with the formation of the imperfect tense occur when one tries to add an ἐ onto a word that already begins with a vowel. As you might expect when this happens certain changes occur: any vowel that can lengthen, will lengthen with the addition of ἐ. So:

- ι, υ and ω remain the same (e.g. ἰσχυω becomes ἰσχυον in the imperfect, thus with these verbs the only indication of the imperfect is the ending);
- α and ε both become η (e.g. ἀγω becomes ἠγον);

- o becomes ω;

- diphthongs behave in a similar way; αι, ει, and οι become ῃ, η and ῳ respectively, and αυ and ευ both become ηὑ.

The task, when looking at an imperfect, is to try and work out what the original stem was before the addition of the ἐ.

Look at Table 8.4 and see if you can work out the original stem of the verbs concerned. The meaning of the stem is given to you so that you can see if you are right when you look it up in a dictionary or on a web page.[2]

Table 8.4

Word	Stem	Basic Meaning of Stem
ἔτυπτον		strike or beat
ἤκουον		hear
ἤλπιζον		hope
ἔσωζον		save
ηὕρισκον		find
ἐζήτουν		seek

Note: the last of these is an example of a contracted verb. This is because the stem ends in an ἐ. An ε followed by ο becomes ου because it is easier to say, for example, ἐζήτουν than ἐζήτεον.

Compound Verbs in the Imperfect Tense

You may remember that back in Chapter 3 we encountered prefixes, i.e. prepositions added to the beginning of a word that change the word's meaning. For example βαλλω, 'I throw' becomes ἀποβαλλω, 'I throw off' when the preposition ἀπο is prefixed to the verb βαλλω. When such prefixes are added to the beginning of verbs they are called compound verbs (because they are made up of a compound of the verb and the preposition).

When compound verbs appear in the imperfect tense, the ἐ is added, not at the beginning of the word, but between the preposition and the verb. For example, ἀποβαλλω becomes ἀπεβαλλον. Notice that the final o of ἀπο has dropped out: this usually happens when the preposition ends in a vowel because it would be hard to say, for example, ἀποεβαλλον.

Prefix	Addition	Stem	Insert	Ending
ἀπ	ε	βαλλ	-	ον

So in order to work out the dictionary form of a compound verb you need to take off the ending, separate the verb from the preposition, remove the ε, rejoin the verb and the preposition and add the first person singular present indicative active ending. This sounds more complicated than it actually is!

Have a go at the examples in Table 8.5 to practise this. This time not only is the first person singular form being used but all three persons, both in the singular and the plural.

Remember that if the *stem* of the verb begins with a vowel, the vowel will change when ε is added. Make sure that you change the vowel back to its original form to find the stem. If, for example, the vowel has changed to a η you will need to check both ε and α in the dictionary to find the original form – you can't tell from the Greek.

In the middle column of Table 8.5 give the first person singular present indicative active form of the verb. The meaning of the verb is given you to help you to check whether you are right.[3]

Note: the last example in Table 8.5 is both a compound verb (preposition at the beginning) and a contracted verb (stem ends with a vowel). See the note on ἐζητουν in the previous section to understand the ending.

Table 8.5

Imperfect Form	1st Person Present Form	Meaning
ἀνηγγελλομεν	ἀναγγελλω	we were reporting
ἀνεβαινετε		you were going up
ἀπεθνησκεν		he was dying
ἀπελυον		I was or they were releasing
κατεκαινετε		you were burning up
περιεπατουν		I was or they were walking about

ADDITIONS AND INSERTS TOGETHER: THE AORIST TENSE

The aorist is, like the imperfect, a past tense. It refers to an action in the past which happens once. Its precise meanings are discussed on p. 151.

A mark of a past tense is that it adds letters at the beginning of a verb stem. In most cases, the aorist, like the imperfect, just adds an ἐ. In addition to adding an ἐ to the beginning of the stem, a σ is inserted between the stem and the ending (like a future verb) when forming the aorist. Finally, distinctive endings are added:

Addition	Stem	Insert	Ending
ἐ	πιστευ	σ	α

Have a look at Table 8.6 to see how this works. The present, the future and the imperfect are listed as well so you can compare them.

To get back to the original stem of an aorist, you need to remove the initial ἐ, the σ insert and the ending that follows it. Don't forget that, like the imperfect, the initial ἐ will have been lengthened if the verb stem starts with a vowel; and that some

Table 8.6

Person	Present Indicative Active	Future Indicative Active	Imperfect Indicative Active	Aorist Indicative Active
1st singular	πιστευω	πιστευσω	ἐπιστευον	ἐπιστευσα
2nd singular	πιστευεις	πιστευσεις	ἐπιστευες	ἐπιστευσας
3rd singular	πιστευει	πιστευσει	ἐπιστευε(ν)	ἐπιστευσε(ν)
1st plural	πιστευομεν	πιστευσομεν	ἐπιστευομεν	ἐπιστευσαμεν
2nd plural	πιστευετε	πιστευσετε	ἐπιστευετε	ἐπιστευσατε
3rd plural	πιστευουσι(ν)	πιστευσουσι(ν)	ἐπιστευον	ἐπιστευσαν

letters change when a σ insert follows them, see pp. 137–8 to remind yourself of these changes.

Bearing this in mind, have a look at the sentences below. The aorists are marked in bold. Work out their first person singular present form and look them up in a dictionary or on a website:[4]

1 οὕτως γὰρ **ἠγάπησεν** ὁ θεὸς τὸν κόσμον,

   thus for he-loved the God the world

(John 3.16)

2 καὶ   εὐθὺς   **ἀνέβλεψεν** καὶ ἠκολούθει αὐτῷ ἐν τῇ ὁδῷ

and immediately he-looked-up and followed   him in the way

(Mark 10.51)

Note: this is a compound verb!

3 Καὶ ὅτε   **ἤγγισαν**   εἰς Ἱεροσόλυμα

and when they-drew-near to Jerusalem

(Matthew 21.1)

Second Aorists

Some verbs in the aorist tense do something unusual. They have ἐ at the beginning but instead of inserting a σ after the stem and having aorist endings, they have the same endings as the imperfect tense, with no σ insert. Also, their stem often changes. So, for example, the aorist of λαμβανω is ἔλαβον (the stem λαμβαν- becomes λαβ-) and the aorist of βαλλω is ἔβαλον (the stem βαλλ- becomes βαλ-). You will find that these verbs are called **second aorist** in some dictionaries and grammars.

If you are working with a dictionary, the only way to tell that these verbs are in the aorist and not the imperfect is from the stem (which, if you try to look it up, you will find does not exist as a proper word). When this happens your dictionary may (but doesn't always) point you to the original form of the word. So if you look up λαβον the dictionary may tell you that it comes from λαμβανω. If you are working with a website or one of the more advanced books for analysing the Greek New Testament, it may give you more information about the different forms your 'problem verb' takes!

ADDITIONS AND INSERTS TOGETHER: THE PERFECT TENSE

The perfect tense refers to an action in the past which affects the present. The precise meaning will be discussed on p. 151 below.

Like the aorist that we have just looked at, the perfect tense has an addition, an insert and its own set of endings. The distinctive features of the perfect are:

- the addition is made up by repeating the first letter of the stem and adding an ἐ

- a κ is inserted between the stem and the ending

- the perfect has its own set of endings

Thus:

Addition	Stem	Insert	Ending
πε	πιστευ	κ	α

Look at Table 8.7 to see what its endings look like.

Some Problems with the Formation of the Perfect

It is very difficult to pronounce some letters when they are doubled (just try saying φεφιληκα). To avoid this, when a verb begins with the letters χ, φ and θ the corresponding hard letter is used when forming the addition to the stem. So χωρεω becomes κεχωρηκα, φιλεω becomes πεφιληκα, and θνησκω becomes τεθνηκα.

Note that the rule governing the lengthening of vowels in contracted verbs still applies, so verbs like φιλεω, whose stem ends with a vowel, undergo a lengthening of that vowel when forming the perfect tense, hence φιλ**ε**ω becomes πεφιλ**η**κα.

Look at the following sentences. The perfect form of the verb is in bold. See if you can work out the stem (and hence the first person singular present indicative active form of the verb), then see if you can find it in a dictionary or on a website:[5]

1 τὰ ῥήματα ἃ ἐγὼ **λελάληκα** ὑμῖν πνεῦμα ἐστιν καὶ

the words which I   I-have-spoken to-you spirit   it-is and

ζωή ἐστιν.

life   it-is

(John 6.63)

Remember: neuter plural nouns sometimes take on verbs in the singular. Here, τὰ ῥήματα is plural but its verb, ἐστιν, is singular.

2 καὶ ἀπάγγειλον αὐτοῖς ὅσα ὁ κύριος σοι **πεποίηκεν**

and announce to-them what the Lord to-you has-done

(Mark 5.19)

3 ὅτι   ὑμεῖς ἐμὲ **πεφιλήκατε** καὶ **πεπιστεύκατε**

because you me   have-loved and   have-believed

(John 16.27)

Try not to be too overwhelmed by the amount of information here. Instead, look along Table 8.7 and see if you can see any patterns that might help you recognize the person of each one

Table 8.7

Person	Present Indicative Active	Future Indicative Active	Imperfect Indicative Active	Aorist Indicative Active	Perfect Indicative Active
1st singular	πιστευω	πιστευσω	ἐπιστευον	ἐπιστευσα	πεπιστευκα
2nd singular	πιστευεις	πιστευσεις	ἐπιστευες	ἐπιστευσας	πεπιστευκας
3rd singular	πιστευει	πιστευσει	ἐπιστευε(ν)	ἐπιστευσε(ν)	πεπιστευκε(ν)
1st plural	πιστευομεν	πιστευσομεν	ἐπιστευομεν	ἐπιστευσαμεν	πεπιστευκαμεν
2nd plural	πιστευετε	πιστευσετε	ἐπιστευετε	ἐπιστευσατε	πεπιστευκατε
3rd plural	πιστευουσι(ν)	πιστευσουσι(ν)	ἐπιστευον	ἐπιστευσαν	πεπιστευκασι(ν)

of these tenses. For example look at the first person plural endings of each tense – do you see anything that they all have in common? Table 8.8 lists some of these common features.

Table 8.8

Person	Characteristic
1st singular	
2nd singular	ends in ς
3rd singular	ends in ε(ν) or ει
1st plural	ends in μεν
2nd plural	ends in τε
3rd plural	sometimes ends in σι(ν)

IRREGULAR VERBS

A number of common verbs are irregular in one or more of their forms. In entirely irregular verbs the past and future forms of the word look so different from the present that you simply cannot work out that they are in any way connected. For example, the aorist of φερω is ἠνεγκον.

Since there are no rules for these irregularities your best strategy is usually guesswork! However, you may find it useful to get to know these very common irregular forms:

- ἠν (she/he/it was) and ἠσαν (they were) are from the past tense of εἰμι (I am). A full chart of the past tense of εἰμι is in the appendix (Table A.12).

- εἶδον (I/they saw) and εἶδεν (she/he/it saw) are from the aorist of ὁράω (I see).

- εἶπον (I said) and εἶπεν (she/he/it said) are from the aorist of λέγω (I say).

- ἐγένετο ('it came to pass') is from the aorist of γίνομαι (I become).

- ἦλθον (I/they came) and ἦλθεν (she/he/it came) are from the aorist of ἔρχομαι (I come).

You will find some of these words in the following passages; they are highlighted in bold. Circle the translation of each in the English text:[6]

1 John 12.41

ταῦτα **εἶπεν** Ἠσαΐας ὅτι **εἶδεν** τὴν δόξαν αὐτοῦ, καὶ ἐλάλησεν περὶ αὐτοῦ.

Isaiah said this because he saw his glory and spoke about him

2 Matthew 22.8

τότε λέγει τοῖς δούλοις αὐτοῦ· ὁ μὲν γάμος ἕτοιμός ἐστιν, οἱ δὲ κεκλημένοι οὐκ **ἦσαν** ἄξιοι·

Then he said to his slaves, "The wedding is ready, but those invited were not worthy"

3 John 1.1

Ἐν ἀρχῇ **ἦν** ὁ λόγος, καὶ ὁ λόγος **ἦν** πρὸς τὸν θεόν, καὶ θεὸς **ἦν** ὁ λόγος.

In the beginning was the Word, and the Word was with God, and the Word was God.

4 John 10.22

Ἐγένετο τότε τὰ ἐγκαίνια ἐν τοῖς Ἱεροσολύμοις, χειμὼν
ἦν,

Then came the Feast of Dedication at Jerusalem. It was winter
(NIV)

5 John 4.46

Ἦλθεν οὖν πάλιν εἰς τὴν Κανὰ τῆς Γαλιλαίας, ὅπου
ἐποίησεν τὸ ὕδωρ οἶνον.

Then he came again to Cana in Galilee where he had changed the
water into wine

When you come across irregular verbs that you do not know,
you will need to find another way of finding the first person
singular present indicative active form of the word. Your dictionary will often, but not always, help (e.g. look up ἤνεγκ ... in
your dictionary and see what it does). Alternatively you will need
to use other tools, such as a website, to help you track the word
down.

THE IMPORTANCE OF THE TENSES AND THEIR MEANINGS

In Greek the present and future tenses have no greater significance than they do in English and are not worth exploring
further. The past tenses, however, are significantly different and
worth exploring here.

- The **imperfect** tense refers to an action which began in the
  past but which may or may not have finished. It is therefore
  normally translated as 'I was . . .', for example, 'I was studying', implying that the studying began in the past but not
  indicating whether it is still happening now or not.

- The **aorist** tense refers to a single action in the past. It is normally translated as, for example, 'I studied' and in Greek implies that this studying happened once and has now finished.

- The **perfect** tense refers to an action in the past which affects the present. It is normally translated as, for example, 'I have studied' implying that previous studying still has an effect in the present time, i.e. if I have studied it in the past, I now know it!

There is another tense as well – the pluperfect. It refers to an action in the past which affected the past and is normally translated as, for example, 'I had studied', implying that previous studying affected a situation in the past. Since the pluperfect is very rarely used in the New Testament, we won't be studying it here.

It is clear that the different nuances that these tenses give to a verb can be highly significant for the theology of a passage. For the same reason, if we misunderstand the tenses used in a passage, we are likely to misinterpret it. Look at the following different uses of the verb γεννάω, which means 'to beget', 'bear a child' or 'bring forth'. Spend some time making sure you are clear about the significance of the different tenses used:

1 ἐν γὰρ Χριστῷ Ἰησοῦ διὰ   τοῦ εὐαγγελίου ἐγὼ ὑμᾶς

in for   Christ Jesus through the   gospel   I   you

ἐγέννησα.

begot/brought forth

(1 Corinthians 4.15)

The verb is first person singular aorist.

Here Paul looks backwards to the one time in the past that he brought forth the Corinthian church to be 'in Christ'.

2 υἱός μου   εἶ   σύ, ἐγὼ σήμερον **γεγέννηκα**   σε.

son of-me you-are you I   today begotten/brought forth you

(Acts 13.33)

The verb is first person singular perfect.

This verse is a quotation from Psalm 2.7 where God addresses the king and says 'today I have begotten you'. The begetting must have happened before God spoke, but the reference to 'today' and the use of the perfect tense for the verb γενναω implies that the begetting still has an effect in the present time; it is as if God is saying that 'I begot you and as a result you are begotten now'.

3 καὶ ἡ γυνή σου Ἐλισάβετ **γεννήσει** υἱόν   σοι

and the wife of-you Elisabeth   will-bear a-son to-you

(Luke 1.13)

The verb is third person singular future.

This refers to a simple action in the future.

SUBJUNCTIVES, IMPERATIVES AND INFINITIVES AGAIN

In Chapter 7 we looked at subjunctives (the indefinite form of the verb, for example, 'I might do this'). The subjunctive only occurs in one other tense: the aorist. Its form is unusual. It has no addition at the start, but instead has a σ insert as if it were a future. It then takes the same endings as the present subjunctive. For example, the subjunctive aorist of πιστευω would look like this: πιστευσω (and so on following the present subjunctive endings).

Similarly, the imperative occurs only in the present and aorist tenses. At first glance it may surprise you that there is an aorist imperative (you can't command someone to do something in the past – it is too late!). But the aorist imperative does not refer to something in the past: instead it refers to the frequency with which something is to be done.

• The present imperative implies a command to do something with no limit on how often it should be done.

• The aorist imperative implies a command to do something once, and only once.

If you want to know what they both look like you can consult the full chart of present and aorist imperatives in the appendix (Table A.16). For now it is enough to have an idea of the difference they make to the translation.

The infinitive occurs in the present and aorist tenses, but also in the perfect tense. As you might expect, the aorist infinitive refers to an action that should happen only once; and the perfect infinitive refers to something past that continues to have effects in the present. Again, it is not necessary to learn these in detail, but only to recognize the significance of different tenses when you come across them.

Look at the following sentences and see if you can see the importance of the different tenses here. You may find some of them surprising:

1 **ἐλθέτω** ἡ βασιλεία σου·

come the kingdom your

(Matthew 6:10)

This is a third person singular aorist imperative.

2   ὅσα   ἔχεις **πώλησον** καὶ **δὸς** [τοῖς] πτωχοῖς, καὶ

whatever you-have   sell   and give to-the poor   and

ἕξεις   θησαυρὸν ἐν οὐρανῷ, καὶ   δεῦρο   **ἀκολούθει**

you-will-have treasure in heaven and come-here   follow

μοι.

me.

(Mark 10.21)

There are three imperatives in this sentence: πώλησον, δὸς and
ἀκολούθει. All of them are second person singular but the first
two are aorists and the third is present.

δὸς looks unusual because it comes from δίδωμι, the verb we
met in Chapter 7, which, like other -μι verbs, has unusual endings.

Note: δεῦρο looks like an imperative in its English translation
but isn't one. It is an interjection or little word used to describe
time (i.e. start here and now!).

3 μὴ **φοβοῦ**, μόνον **πίστευε**

not fear   only   believe

φοβου and πίστευε are both second person singular present
imperatives.

4 οὐ μόνον τὸ **ποιῆσαι** ἀλλὰ καὶ τὸ **θέλειν**

not only   to-do   but also   to-desire

(2 Corinthians 8.10)

θελειν is a present infinitive (continuous action); ποιῆσαι an
aorist infinitive (single action).

5 καὶ λιθάσαντες τὸν Παῦλον ἔσυρον ἔξω τῆς πόλεως

and having-stoned   Paul dragged out-from the   city

νομίζοντες αὐτὸν **τεθνηκέναι.**

believing   him   to-have-died

(Acts 14.19)

τεθνηκέναι is a perfect infinitive: Paul has already died and continues to be dead!

LOOKING AT TRANSLATIONS

Remembering the importance of tenses, look at the following sentence with its accompanying translation:

ἀπεκρίθη αὐτῷ Σίμων Πέτρος· κύριε, πρὸς τίνα

answered he Simon Peter Lord to whom

ἀπελευσόμεθα; ῥήματα ζωῆς αἰωνίου ἔχεις, καὶ ἡμεῖς

go-away   words of-life eternal have and we

πεπιστεύκαμεν καὶ ἐγνώκαμεν ὅτι σὺ εἶ ὁ ἅγιος τοῦ

believe   and   know   that you are the holy of-the

θεοῦ. ἀπεκρίθη αὐτοῖς ὁ Ἰησοῦς· οὐκ ἐγὼ ὑμᾶς τοὺς

God answered they the Jesus   not I you the

δώδεκα ἐξελεξάμην;

twelve   choose

(John 6.68–70)

Look at the following verbs from this passage and make sure you can translate them (i.e. if they are third person singular you need to add a he/she/it etc.). As you can see, some have irregular forms and some occur in a form that you have not yet met. We will be meeting these forms in the next chapter.

ἀπεκρίθη	third person singular aorist of ἀποκρινομαι, 'to answer'
ἀπελευσόμεθα	first person plural future of ἀπέρχομαι, 'to go away'
ἔχεις	second person singular present of ἔχω, 'to have'
πεπιστεύκαμεν	first person plural perfect of πιστευω, 'to believe'
ἐγνώκαμεν	first person plural perfect of γινωσκω, 'to know'
ἐξελεξάμην	first person plural aorist of ἐκλέγομαι, 'to choose'

Now look at the following translations and decide which you think is the best. Remember to ask yourself questions such as, which words have been added? which words have been missed out? etc. to help you make a decision.

Simon Peter answered him, "Lord, to whom would we go? You have the words that give eternal life. And now we believe and know that you are the Holy One who has come from God." Jesus replied, "I chose the twelve of you, didn't I?" (GNB)

Simon Peter answered him, "Lord, to whom shall we go? You have the words of eternal life. We believe and know that you are the Holy One of God." Then Jesus replied, "Have I not chosen you, the Twelve?" (NIV)

But Simon Peter answered Him, "Lord, to whom shall we go? You have the words of eternal life. Also we have come to believe and know that You are the Christ, the Son of the living God." Jesus answered them, "Did I not choose you, the twelve . . ." (NKJV)

REVIEW OF LEARNING

In this chapter we have looked at:

- how verbs are formed into different tenses by adding letters to the stem and changing the endings;

- how to recognize future, imperfect, aorist and perfect tenses;

- how the different tenses are used to give different shades of meaning;

- common irregular verbs;

- subjunctives and imperatives in the aorist tense; infinitives in the aorist and perfect tenses.

Notes

1 Your table should look like this:

Verb	Basic stem	Tense	Person	Meaning
ἀκουσεις	ἀκου-	future	2nd sing.	you will hear
θεραπευετε	θεραπευ-	present	2nd plural	you heal
βασιλευσει	βασιλευ-	future	3rd sing.	she/he/it will rule
θεραπευσω	θεραπευ-	future	1st sing.	I will heal
ἀκουομεν	ἀκου-	present	1st plural	we hear
βασιλευουσιν	βασιλευ-	present	3rd plural	they rule

2 Your table should look like this:

Word	Stem	Basic Meaning of Stem
ἔτυπτον	τυπτ-	strike or beat
ἤκουον	ακου-	hear
ἤλπιζον	ἐλπιζ-	hope
ἔσωζον	σώζ-	save
ηὗρισκον	εὑρισκ-	find
ἐζητουν	ζητε-	seek

3 Your answers (from top to bottom) should be: ἀναβαινω, ἀποθνῃσκω, ἀπολυω, κατακαιω, περιπατεω.

4 (1) ἀγαπαω, (2) ἀναβλεπω, (3) ἐγγιζω.

5 (1) λαλεω, (2) ποιεω, (3) φιλεω and πιστευω.

6 (1) he (Isaiah) said, he saw; (2) they (those invited) were; (3) it (the Word) was (three times); (4) it (the Feast of Dedication) came, it was; (5) he came.

9

Voice: Active, Passive and Middle

In Chapter 7 we began looking at verbs. We saw that the endings indicate **person** – who is doing the action (I, you, she/he/it, etc.).We also looked at the different **moods** of a verb: the indicative (which describes a definite action), the subjunctive (which expresses uncertainty), the imperative (which turns the verb into a command) and the infinitive (which makes a general statement). In Chapter 8 we looked at the different **tenses** of a verb: present and future (which are both self-explanatory), the imperfect (which refers to an action that began in the past but may or may not have finished), the aorist (which refers to an action in the past that happened once) and the perfect (which refers to an action in the past that still affects the present).

A final layer of meaning in a verb is known in dictionaries and grammars as the **voice** of a verb. There are two voices that will be familiar to us – the active and the passive voices. In this chapter we will be looking at the difference between the two and also exploring an oddity in New Testament Greek, the middle voice, which is a remnant of earlier classical Greek but which has, by and large, lost its original meaning.

WHOSE STANDPOINT?

The verbs that we have been looking at so far all have someone or something (the subject) doing the verb. For example: John baptized Jesus in the river Jordan. This situation is being described from the standpoint of the 'do-er', so John (the subject of the sentence) does the baptizing. The verb is therefore 'active'.

It is, however, also possible to say the same thing from the standpoint of the person 'being done to'. This sentence is, in effect, a mirror-image of the previous one: Jesus was baptized by John in the river Jordan. It means exactly the same as the first one but this time the subject is Jesus and he is not *doing* the baptizing but is *being* baptized. The verb is therefore 'passive'.

In English, we reflect this change of standpoint by adding a form of the verb 'to be': 'I *am* baptized' (as opposed to 'I baptize'), 'you *were* baptized' (as opposed to 'you baptized'), 'they *will be* baptized' (as opposed to 'they will baptize') etc. In Greek, the passive is reflected by different endings to the verb, and in the case of some of the tenses, different additions to the stem.

If we translate the examples above into Greek, they look like this:

Ἰωαννης ἐβαπτισεν Ἰησουν εἰς τον Ἰορδανην

John   baptized   Jesus   in   the (river) Jordan

Ἰησοῦς ἐβαπτίσθη ὑπὸ Ἰωάννου εἰς τὸν Ἰορδάνην

Jesus was-baptized by   John   in   the (river) Jordan

It is important that you know what active and passive verbs look like in English before you try too hard with the Greek. So practise this by trying to work out whether the verbs in bold in the following sentences are active or passive.[1] Some sentences have a mixture of active and passive – you will need to work out which is which:

1 Luke 10.22: All things **have been handed over** to me by my Father;

2 Mark 4.21: He said to them, 'Is a lamp brought in to **be put under** the bushel basket, or under the bed, and not on the lampstand?'

3 John 14.21: and those who love me **will be loved** by my Father, and **I will love** them and **reveal** myself to them.

4 Luke 21.16: You **will be betrayed** even by parents and brothers, by relatives and friends; and they **will put** some of you to death.

Once you have worked out which of the verbs are passive go back and work out which noun or pronoun is the **subject** of each passive verb.[2]

When we use a verb in the passive voice in an English sentence, we indicate who is doing the action with the word 'by'. For example, in number 1 above, the subject is 'all things' but it is the father ('by my Father') who has done the 'handing over'.

Greek does a similar thing. Just as in English the 'do-er' is indicated by the word 'by', in Greek the person or thing who does the action is marked by the word ὑπο (by), followed by the genitive case.

Look at Luke 10.22 in Greek to see how this works:

πάντα   μοι   παρεδόθη   **ὑπὸ τοῦ πατρός μου,**

all-things to-me have-been-handed-over by   the   father of-me.

This is worth knowing, as it is an easy way to spot a passive in Greek. If the 'do-er' is identified, they will appear in the genitive with the preposition ὑπο. Remember, however, that ὑπο can also mean 'under' when it is followed by an accusative instead of the genitive. Remember also that the 'do-er' is not always identified. For example, in number 2 above, the lamp may 'be put under' the bushel by anybody – we are not told who.

RECOGNIZING PASSIVES

Indicatives

In the previous two chapters we looked at all the forms of the active verb and noted 'tell-tale' characteristics that helped us to identify the tense, mood and person of the verb. For example:

- There were some basic characteristics for the endings.

- All regular verbs in the future tense had a σ after the stem and before the ending.

- The second person plural form usually ended in -τε.

- Verbs in the subjunctive mood had a lengthened vowel (η or ω) in the ending.

As we turn to the passive forms, we will find once again that there are distinctive markers that give us a clue to the tense, mood or person of a verb. We will also find signs that tell us these verbs are not in the active voice. Have a look at the summary of the passive indicative forms in Table 9.1.

Some of these forms are purely theoretical: for example, πιστευω doesn't occur in the Greek New Testament in the future passive indicative form. They are listed here simply to give you the idea of what they would look like if they did occur.

As before don't even try to remember all of these, instead look for any patterns that you can see. You will see that:

- The ending -μαι often marks the first person singular.

- The ending -ομεθα often marks the first person plural.

- The ending -εσθε often marks the second person plural.

- The ending -ονται often marks the third person plural.

Also, look back at the summary of the active indicative forms in Chapter 8 and see in what ways they are similar. Some of the patterns you may identify are given below:

- The same rule applies for additions (ἐ or a repetition of the first letter of the verb plus ε) in the imperfect, aorist and perfect tenses as applied for the active voice.

- Inserts are, however, different to those used in the active voice. To form the future tense, instead of just inserting a σ you need

Table 9.1

Person	Present Indicative Passive	Future Indicative Passive	Imperfect Indicative Passive	Aorist Indicative Passive	Perfect Indicative Passive
1st sing.	πιστευομαι	πιστευθησομαι	ἐπιστευομην	ἐπιστευθην	πεπιστευμαι
2nd sing.	πιστευη	πιστευθηση	ἐπιστευου	ἐπιστευθης	πεπιστευσαι
3rd sing.	πιστευεται	πιστευθησεται	ἐπιστευετο	ἐπιστευθη	πεπιστευται
1st plural	πιστευομεθα	πιστευθησομεθα	ἐπιστευομεθα	ἐπιστευθημεν	πεπιστευμεθα
2nd plural	πιστευεσθε	πιστευθησεσθε	ἐπιστευεσθε	ἐπιστευθητε	πεπιστευσθε
3rd plural	πιστευονται	πιστευθησονται	ἐπιστευοντο	ἐπιστευθησαν	πεπιστευνται

to insert θησ. To form the aorist, you need to insert θ instead of σ:

	Addition	Stem	Insert	Ending
Future	-	**πιστευ**	**θησ**	**ομαι**
Aorist	**ἐ**	**πιστευ**	**θ**	**ην**

Putting it into Practice

As the passive is not as common as the active form of the verb, it is not as important that you are able to recognize it. What is important, however, is that when you discover from a website or dictionary that something is a passive, you will be able to translate it.

Look at the following sentences. After each, you will be given the details of the verb in bold that you need to know. Practise translating the verbs as passives, so you are clear how to do it. You can check your answers in a Bible.[3]

1 μόνον πίστευσον, καὶ **σωθήσεται**.

   only   believe   and

(Luke 8.50)

σωθήσεται is the third person singular future passive of σωζω, 'I save'.

2 Ἡρῴδης **ἐταράχθη** καὶ πᾶσα Ἰεροσόλυμα μετ' αὐτοῦ,

   Herod   and all   Jerusalem with him

(Matthew 2.3)

ἐταραχθη is the third person singular aorist passive of ταρασσω, 'I disturb'.

3 σὺ εἶ Σίμων ὁ υἱὸς Ἰωάννου, σὺ **κληθήσῃ** Κηφᾶς,

  you are Simon   son   John   you   Cephas

(John 1.42)

κληθήσῃ is the second person singular future passive of καλεω, 'I call'.

4 ὅταν γὰρ ἐκ   νεκρῶν ἀναστῶσιν οὔτε γαμοῦσιν οὔτε

  when for from (the) dead   rise   neither marry   nor

γαμίζονται,

(Mark 12.25)

γαμίζονται is the third person plural present passive of γαμιζω, 'I give (a bride) in marriage'.

5 γυμνιτεύομεν καὶ **κολαφιζόμεθα** καὶ ἀστατοῦμεν

  naked   and   and homeless

(1 Corinthians 4.11)

κολαφιζομεθα is the first person plural present passive of κολαφιζω, 'I beat'.

Imperatives and Infinitives

Passive imperatives and infinitives (Table 9.2) look a little like their other passive counterparts. Also note that, as with active verbs, there are no imperfect or future imperatives or infinitives.

As with the other forms just notice any patterns that you see emerging. In particular notice that:

- With the exception of the second person singular, the present passive imperative and infinitive is formed with -εσθ before the endings.

Table 9.2

Imperative	Present Passive	Aorist Passive	Perfect Passive
2nd singular	πιστευου	πιστευθητι	
3rd singular	πιστευεσθω	πιστευθητω	
2nd plural	πιστευεσθε	πιστευθητε	
3rd plural	πιστευεσθωσαν	πιστευθητωσαν	
Infinitive	πιστευεσθαι	πιστευθηναι	πεπιστευσθαι

- The aorist passive imperative and infinitive, like the active, have no ε addition before the stem.

- The insert for the aorist passive imperative and infinitive is, as for the indicative, θ.

- All the infinitives end with αι.

Practise on the following sentences. The passive imperative or infinitive is given in bold in the Greek text; the English word in brackets underneath is the dictionary meaning of the stem. Work out how the word should be translated, and check your answers in your English New Testament.[4]

1 Μὴ **ταρασσέσθω** ὑμῶν ἡ καρδία· πιστεύετε εἰς τὸν θεὸν

   not   (disturb)   of-you the heart;

   καὶ εἰς ἐμὲ πιστεύετε.

(John 14.1)

You are probably able to translate the second half of this sentence without any help!

2 καὶ   συνήρχοντο   ὄχλοι πολλοὶ ἀκούειν καὶ **θεραπεύεσθαι**
and were-gathering crowds many   hear   and   (heal)

ἀπὸ τῶν ἀσθενειῶν αὐτῶν·
from   sicknesses   their

(Luke 5.15)

Can you also identify an active infinitive in this passage?

3 καὶ ἐκτείνας τὴν χεῖρα ἥψατο αὐτοῦ λέγων· θέλω,
and stretching the hand touched him   saying, 'I-wish,

καθαρίσθητι· καὶ   εὐθέως ἐκαθαρίσθη αὐτοῦ ἡ λέπρα.
(clean)'   and immediately clean   of-him the leprosy

(Matthew 8.3)

Can you also identify an aorist indicative passive in this sentence?

4 Πάτερ ἡμῶν ὁ ἐν τοῖς οὐρανοῖς· **ἁγιασθήτω** τὸ ὄνομα σου·
Father our who in the heavens, (consecrate) the name your

(Matthew 6.9)

5 εἶπεν **φωνηθῆναι** αὐτῷ τοὺς δούλους τούτους
he-said (call)   to-him the servants these

(Luke 19.15)

6 αἱ γυναῖκες ἐν ταῖς ἐκκλησίαις σιγάτωσαν· οὐ γὰρ

   the women in the   churches keep silence; not for

ἐπιτρέπεται αὐταῖς λαλεῖν, ἀλλὰ **ὑποτασσέσθωσαν**,

   permitted   to-them speak,   but (command obedience)

(1 Corinthians 14.34)

Notice that as well as the third person plural passive imperative, there is a third person plural active imperative. There is also an active infinitive. Identify both of these words.

A STRANGE LEFTOVER FROM CLASSICAL GREEK: THE MIDDLE VOICE

The Meaning of the Middle

In English we are used to active and passive forms of the verb. In addition, Greek has a third form – the **middle** – and it is something of an anomaly.

When the middle was used in classical Greek, by and large it had a kind of reflexive form, that is, I do something (or let something happen) to myself. So 'I wash myself' would have been in the middle voice in classical Greek. But New Testament Greek is a later, much less sophisticated form of Greek: although the form of the middle remains, in most cases its meaning is not distinct.

So by the time of the New Testament, the middle voice had largely dropped out of common usage. Most of the verbs in the middle voice that you will come across in New Testament Greek actually have a normal, active meaning. For example, the verb ἔρχομαι, which means 'I come' and which occurs regularly in the New Testament, has a middle form but an active meaning. You will also come across verbs that have an active form in the present tense but a middle form in one of their other tenses, for example, γινώσκω (I know) is in the active voice in the present tense but in the middle voice in the future tense – γνώσομαι (I will know). Although the forms are odd, translating these verbs is quite straightforward. A few of them are very common, so later in the chapter we will give them some attention.

First, however, we will look at the (relatively rare) occasions when a typical verb with an active meaning is used reflexively, that is, in the middle voice.

The Form of the Middle

In the present, imperfect and perfect tenses the middle forms of the verb are exactly the same as the passive forms; refer back to Table 9.1 to remind yourself of these. This means that Bible scholars sometimes need to use their judgement about whether to translate a word with a passive or a middle meaning.

In the future and aorist tenses, the middle has its own forms, which are shown in Tables 9.3 and 9.4. Table 9.3 shows the future and aorist middle indicative forms of the verb πιστευω. The passive forms of these tenses have also been included so that you can compare passive and middle and spot the differences. In Table 9.4 you will find the forms of the aorist imperative and infinitive (remember that the future doesn't have these forms).

Things to notice from Tables 9.3 and 9.4 are:

- Both future and aorist middle forms of the verb have **inserts** like the active but different **endings**. For example:

Addition	Stem	Insert	Ending
ε	πιστευ	σ	αμην

- Though the insert for the future middle is the same as for the future active (-σ not θησ) the **endings** of the future middle are the same as for the future passive.

- The endings of the aorist middle are quite like the imperfect passive (and middle) endings.

Table 9.3

Future Middle Indicative	Future Passive Indicative	Aorist Middle Indicative	Aorist Passive Indicative
πιστευσομαι	πιστευθησομαι	ἐπιστευσαμην	ἐπιστευθην
πιστευση	πιστευθηση	ἐπιστευσω	ἐπιστευθης
πιστευσεται	πιστευθησεται	ἐπιστευσατο	ἐπιστευθη
πιστευσομεθα	πιστευθησομεθα	ἐπιστευσαμεθα	ἐπιστευθημεν
πιστευσεσθε	πιστευθησεσθε	ἐπιστευσασθε	ἐπιστευθητε
πιστευσονται	πιστευθησονται	ἐπιστευσαντο	ἐπιστευθησαν

Table 9.4

Aorist Middle Imperative	
2nd singular	πιστευσαι
3rd singular	πιστευσασθω
2nd plural	πιστευσασθε
3rd plural	πιστευσασθωσαν
Aorist Middle Infinitive	πιστευσασθαι

Practice Translating the Middle Form

In the examples below, all the verbs in bold have a 'middle', reflexive meaning – in the English translation this might be expressed by a term such as 'myself' or 'himself' etc. Translate these verbs: the root meaning in English is given in brackets underneath to help you. Then add in words in the accompanying English translation that reflect the translation you have arrived at.[5] For example:

1 Τότε ὁ Ἰησοῦς εἶπεν τοῖς μαθηταῖς αὐτοῦ· εἴ

   then   Jesus said   disciples   his   if

τις   θέλει ὀπίσω μου ἐλθεῖν, **ἀπαρνησάσθω** ἑαυτὸν

someone wishes after me to-come,   (deny)   himself

                                       (Matthew 16.24)

Answer: Then Jesus said to His disciples, 'If anyone wishes to come after Me, *let him deny* himself . . .' (NAS). ἀπαρνησάσθω is third person singular, aorist middle imperative. In this case, the reflexive character of the verb is made very clear by the use of the reflexive pronoun, ἑαυτον.

2   ῥίψας   τὰ ἀργύρια εἰς τὸν ναὸν ἀνεχώρησεν, καὶ

   throwing-down the silver   in the temple departed,   and

ἀπελθὼν **ἀπήγξατο.**

  went   (hang)

                                       (Matthew 27.5)

throwing down the pieces of silver in the temple, he departed; and he went and . . . .

3 Πάλαι   δοκεῖτε ὅτι ὑμῖν **ἀπολογούμεθα**

All-this-time think that to-you   (defend)

(2 Corinthians 12.19)

have you been thinking all along that .... before you?

4 εἶπεν δὲ πρὸς αὐτούς· ὁρᾶτε καὶ **φυλάσσεσθε** ἀπὸ

said and to   them watch and   (guard) against

πάσης πλεονεξίας,

all   greed

(Luke 12.15)

and he said to them, 'Take care! Watch and .... against all kinds of greed.'

5 Σταυρώσαντες δὲ αὐτὸν **διεμερίσαντο** τὰ ἱμάτια αὐτοῦ

having-crucified and him   (divide)   the clothes of-him

βάλλοντες κλῆρον,

casting   a-lot

(Matthew 27.35)

and having crucified him, ... his clothes by casting a lot

Middle Form with Active Meaning

As already mentioned, some verbs in Greek take a middle (or sometimes passive) *form*, but have an active *meaning*. These are found more often than true middles in the New Testament, and some are very common words indeed. In some commentaries you will find these referred to as 'deponent' verbs. For example:

ἀποκρινομαι	I answer
ἀρχομαι	I begin
γινομαι	I become
δυναμαι	I am able
ἐρχομαι	I come
πορευομαι	I go
προσευχομαι	I pray
φοβεομαι	I fear

Most of these words can also take prefixes to form compound verbs, forming words like ἐκπορευομαι (go out) and συνερχομαι (gather together).

Practice Translating Active Verbs with a Middle Form

In the following sentences, identify the verbs in bold type by consulting the list of verbs above. Note that some of them are compound verbs. Then translate them, and put each sentence into good English. Check your answers in an English translation of the New Testament:[6]

1 Ἄγε νῦν οἱ λέγοντες· σήμερον ἢ αὔριον **πορευσόμεθα**
come now (you) who-say   today   or tomorrow

εἰς τήνδε τὴν πόλιν
to   this   city
(James 4.13)

2 καὶ ἀπολύσας τοὺς ὄχλους ἀνέβη εἰς τὸ ὄρος
and sending-away the crowd he-went-up into   mountain

κατ' ἰδίαν **προσεύξασθαι**.
by himself
(Matthew 14.23)

3 γάλα ὑμᾶς ἐπότισα, οὐ   βρῶμα·   οὔπω γὰρ **ἐδύνασθε**.

  milk you I-gave   not (solid) food, not-yet for

ἀλλ᾽ οὐδὲ ἔτι νῦν **δύνασθε**,

but not-even now

(1 Corinthians 3.2)

As you know, there are no separate middle forms for the present tense. The last word, therefore, has a passive/middle form, although it has an active meaning.

LOOKING AT TRANSLATIONS

ὁ παλαιὸς ἡμῶν ἄνθρωπος   συνεσταυρώθη, ἵνα

the   old   of-us person (literally 'man') crucify   so-that

καταργηθῇ τὸ σῶμα τῆς ἁμαρτίας, τοῦ   μηκέτι

  abolish   the body of-the   sin, in-order-that no-longer

δουλεύειν ἡμᾶς τῇ ἁμαρτίᾳ· ὁ   γὰρ ἀποθανὼν

be-enslaved we to-the sin   the-one for dying

δεδικαίωται   ἀπὸ τῆς ἁμαρτίας. εἰ δὲ ἀπεθάνομεν σὺν

make-righteous from the   sin   if but we-died   with

Χριστῷ, πιστεύομεν ὅτι καὶ συζήσομεν αὐτῷ,

Christ   believe   that also live   with-him

(Romans 6.6–8)

Look at the following verbs from the above passage, check them against your charts and see if you can work out what form they are and therefore what they should mean. The first person present indicative active form (i.e. the dictionary form) of each verb has been given to help you.

συνεσταυρώθη (συνσταυρόω) – this is a compound verb which in the aorist adds a ν before the insert ε.

καταργηθῇ (καταργέω)

δεδικαίωται (δικαιόω)

ἀπεθάνομεν (ἀποθνήσκω) – this is an irregular verb so miss it out if you like. If you want to work it out it is an aorist with imperfect looking endings.

πιστεύομεν (πιστεύω)

συζήσομεν (συζάω)

Here are some questions to remind you of what you need to discover about each verb:

- What person is it (first, second or third, singular or plural)?
- What voice is it (active, passive or middle)?
- What mood is it (indicative, subjunctive, imperative or infinitive)?
- What tense is it (present, future, imperfect, aorist or perfect)?

Remember to ask what difference the tenses make to the meaning of the passage.

Now look at the following translations and decide which you think is the best. Remember to ask yourself questions such as, which words have been added and which words have been missed out? to help you make a decision.

our old being has been put to death with Christ on his cross, in order that the power of the sinful self might be destroyed, so that we should no longer be the slaves of sin. For when people die, they are set free from the power of sin. Since we have died with Christ, we believe that we will also live with him. (GNB)

our old self was crucified with him so that the body of sin might be done away with, that we should no longer be slaves to sin –

because anyone who has died has been freed from sin. Now if we died with Christ, we believe that we will also live with him (NIV).

our old man was crucified with Him, that the body of sin might be done away with, that we should no longer be slaves of sin. For he who has died has been freed from sin. Now if we died with Christ, we believe that we shall also live with Him (NKJ)

REVIEW OF LEARNING

In this chapter we have looked at:

• whose standpoint? Active and passive ways to describe the action;

• how to recognize passive forms of verbs, and how to translate them;

• the middle voice: its meaning and translation.

Notes

1 (1) passive, (2) passive, (3) passive, active, active, (4) passive, active.
2 (1) all things, (2) a lamp, (3) those who love me, (4) you.
3 (1) he/she/it shall be saved; in this verse, the context indicates it should be 'she shall be saved'; (2) (he) was disturbed; (3) you shall be called; (4) (they) shall be given in marriage; (5) we are beaten.
4 (1) let it (not) be disturbed; the second half of the sentence should read 'believe in God and believe in me'; (2) to be healed; the active infinitive is ἀκουειν, 'to hear'; (3) be clean; the aorist indicative passive is ἐκαθαρίσθη, 'it was cleansed'. Note that the emphasis has shifted from the man to the leprosy in this second half of the verse. (4) may it be consecrated; (5) to be called; (6) let them be placed under obedience; the third person plural passive imperative is σιγάτωσαν 'let them keep silence'; the active infinitive is λαλειν, 'to speak'.
5 (2) hanged himself, (third person singular aorist middle indicative); (3) we have been defending ourselves, (first person plural present middle indicative); (4) guard yourselves (second person plural present middle

imperative), (5) they divided amongst themselves (third person plural aorist middle indicative).

6 (1) we shall go (first person plural future middle indicative); (2) to pray (aorist middle infinitive); (3) you were (not) able (second person plural imperfect middle indicative), you are (not) able (second person plural present middle indicative).

10

Participles and the Articular Infinitive

In the previous chapters we have explored the different forms a verb can take in New Testament Greek. There is still one form the verb can take which we haven't looked at yet which will be the main topic for this chapter. This is the **participle**, which is common in English, but which is even more important and useful in Greek.

In addition, we will explore a different way that Greek uses the infinitive called the **articular infinitive**. Although we have looked at the normal use of the infinitive, this other, very common, use deserves a mention of its own.

WHAT ARE PARTICIPLES?

Participles in English are often described as '...ing' words (i.e. words which end in '...ing', for example, 'believing', 'talking', etc.). In fact these '...ing' words are the *present active* form of the participle. For example:

   ***Turning** to them, Jesus said . . .   (Luke 23.28)

There are also forms in English for *past* tenses and for the *passive* voice. Here are some examples:

   *. . . and **having heard** them arguing with one another . . .

                                      (Mark 12.28)

'Having heard' is in the past tense and active.

> ***Being abused**, he did not abuse in turn . . .   (1 Peter 2.23)

'Being abused' is in the present tense and passive.

> *. . . the events **having been fulfilled** among us   (Luke 1.1)

'Having been fulfilled' is in the past tense and passive.

We can see this distinction very clearly in the following list:

believing	present active
having believed	past active (aorist or perfect in Greek)
being believed	present passive
having been believed	past passive (aorist or perfect in Greek)

In English translation, these differences are often difficult to spot, and the participle itself may be turned into a different form of the verb (for example, compare the translations of the passages given above with the NRSV or another translation[1]). But in Greek the form of the participle carries specific information and tends to be used more precisely.

In Greek, participles have a particular and very important role. Technically they are known as 'verbal adjectives' because they fall halfway between verbs and adjectives. They can be used to describe a verb (like an adverb) or a noun (like an adjective). In Greek therefore:

- They share some of the characteristics of *verbs* in that they can appear in different tenses (present, aorist or perfect) and in different voices (active or passive).

- They share some of the characteristics of *adjectives* and have a case (nominative, accusative, genitive or dative); number (singular or plural) and gender (masculine, feminine or neuter).

This means that to understand the meaning of a participle we must look at its behaviour as a verb (tense and voice) as well as its behaviour as an adjective (case, number and gender). We will examine each of these aspects in turn.

CHARACTERISTICS OF GREEK PARTICIPLES

Tenses

Participles can occur in three different tenses:

- present
- aorist
- perfect

As usual, the aorist tense indicates a single action in the past and the perfect tense indicates an action in the past which affects the present. Unfortunately, the English language doesn't allow us to distinguish between these two (a problem for translators of the New Testament into English!).

The use of tenses in Greek is particularly important and worth being aware of. A key feature of Greek participles is that the choice of tense is governed by when the action of the participle takes place *in relation to the main verb*.

In Greek, the *present* participle is used when the action that the participle refers to takes place *at the same time* as the action in the main verb. For example:

ὁ **πιστεύων** εἰς τὸν υἱὸν ἔχει ζωὴν αἰώνιον

the-one **believing** into the son   has   eternal   life

(John 3.36)

Here, 'believing' takes place *at the same time* as having eternal life, so πιστεύων is in the present tense.

ὅτι **βλέποντες** οὐ βλέπουσιν καὶ **ἀκούοντες** οὐκ ἀκούουσιν

because **seeing** not they-see and **hearing** not they-hear

(Matthew 13.13)

βλέποντες and ἀκούοντες are in the present tense. This means that they are taking place *at the same time* as the not seeing and the not hearing.

In Greek a *past* participle (either perfect or aorist) is used when the action that the participle refers to takes place *before* the action of the main verb. For example:

Ἀκούσαντες δὲ   οἱ ἐν Ἱεροσολύμοις ἀπόστολοι ὅτι

having-heard but those in   Jerusalem   apostles that

δέδεκται   ἡ Σαμάρεια τὸν λόγον τοῦ θεοῦ, ἀπέστειλαν

had-received the Samaria the word of God, they-sent

πρὸς αὐτοὺς Πέτρον καὶ Ἰωάννην,

to   them   Peter and John

(Acts 8.14)

In this example the apostles in Jerusalem heard that Samaria had received the word of God *before* they sent Peter and John and so the participle is in the aorist.

ἔλεγεν   οὖν ὁ Ἰησοῦς πρὸς τοὺς **πεπιστευκότας** αὐτῷ

he-said therefore Jesus to   the **having-believed** in-him

Ἰουδαίους·

Jews

(John 8.31)

In this example the Jews had begun to believe in Jesus in the past, but are still believing in him at the time Jesus is speaking. So the participle is in the perfect tense.

Voice

Like a verb, a participle may have an active, middle or passive meaning. There is nothing new or complicated about the way the different voices work for participles. Here is an example, by way of an illustration:

εἰ δὲ τὸν χόρτον τοῦ ἀγροῦ σήμερον ὄντα καὶ αὔριον

if but the   flower of-the field   today   being and tomorrow

εἰς κλίβανον **βαλλόμενον**

into an-oven **being-thrown**

(Matthew 6.30)

Number, Gender and Case

One of the problems when using participles in English is knowing which noun or pronoun they go with. See, for example, the following made-up sentence:

Jesus said to the disciples sitting in the boat . . .

In English it is not altogether clear who is sitting in the boat: is it Jesus or the disciples?

In Greek this problem does not arise because the case, number and gender of the participle always matches that of the noun it describes. So, if the noun is a nominative masculine singular, the participle will be as well. If the noun is an accusative feminine plural, so will the participle be, and so on.

The sentence above could be written like this:

Ἰησους εἶπεν τοις μαθηταις **καθημενος** ἐν τῳ πλοιῳ

Jesus   said   to-the disciples   sitting   in the boat

Here καθημενος is nominative singular, so it is clear that it is Jesus, the subject of the sentence, who is sitting in the boat.

Alternatively, it could be written like this:

'Iησους εἶπεν τοις μαθηταις **καθημενοις** ἐν τῳ πλοιῳ

Since καθημενοις, like μαθηταις, is in the dative plural, it is clear that it is the disciples who are sitting in the boat.

THE USES OF THE PARTICIPLE

Participles have various uses, but as already noted, a participle's main function is as a 'verbal adjective'; it tells us more about a noun or pronoun (like an adjective) or more about the verb (like an adverb). In this section we will look at what this means in practice: how they are used and translated.

Participles as Adjectives

We have already seen this aspect of a participle at work. Remember how the participle 'sitting' was used in the phrase 'Jesus said to the disciples sitting in the boat . . . '

This is the simple use of the participle as an adjective; the word 'sitting' tells us more about the noun it relates to. But as with other adjectives, a participle can also be used to stand in for a noun. For example:

ὁ   πιστεύων εἰς αὐτὸν οὐ κρίνεται· ὁ δὲ   μὴ
the (one) believing in him not is-judged; the (one) not

πιστεύων ἤδη   κέκριται,
believing already is-judged

(John 3.18)

Here, ὁ πιστεύων is the subject of the sentence. πιστεύων is a nominative singular masculine participle that takes the place of a noun. This is a very common use of the participle indeed, and is worth bearing in mind.

Participles as Adverbs

As well as telling us something more about nouns, participles can also tell us more about verbs.

In particular, they can tell us *when an event takes place* in relation to the main verb. Again, we have seen examples of this above. It is difficult to make the distinction between the tenses in English, and to do so we often need to supply some extra words. For example, take a look at the following sentence:

καὶ ἰδοὺ δύο τυφλοὶ **καθήμενοι** παρὰ τὴν ὁδόν
and behold two blind (men) sitting   by   the road

ἀκούσαντες ὅτι Ἰησοῦς παράγει, ἔκραξαν
having-heard that Jesus passes-by cried-out

(Matthew 20.30)

Here the blind men were sitting by the road when they cried out, but they heard that Jesus passed by before they cried out. In English we might want to indicate this with the words 'as' and 'when' or 'after', for example:

As two blind men were sitting by the road, *when* (or *after*) they heard that Jesus was passing by, they cried out.

In fact we would probably make this into two sentences.

Two blind men were sitting by the road. *When* they heard that Jesus was passing by, they cried out.

Participles can also tell us *the cause of something*. Again in English we need to add an extra word (such as 'because') to draw attention to this. For example:

καὶ πάντες ἐφοβοῦντο αὐτὸν μὴ **πιστεύοντες** ὅτι
and   all   feared   him   not   believing   that

ἐστὶν μαθητής.
he-is a-disciple

(Acts 9.26)

In English we might translate this as:

> And they all feared him *because* they did not believe that he was a disciple.

Have a look at the following sentences with the participles marked in bold. Put them into English in a way which preserves the sense of the participle (i.e. make it clear what tense the participle is in). To help you, the tense of the participle is given to you:[2]

1 καὶ **ἀκούσαντες** οἱ μαθηταὶ ἔπεσαν ἐπὶ πρόσωπον
  and **having-heard** the disciples   fell   on the-face

  αὐτῶν καὶ   ἐφοβήθησαν σφόδρα.
  of-them and they-were-afraid greatly

  (Matthew 17.6)

ἀκούσαντες is aorist here.

2 **βλέπων** δὲ τὸν ἄνεμον ἰσχυρὸν ἐφοβήθη
  seeing but the wind   mighty he-was-afraid

  (Matthew 14.30)

βλέπων is present.

3 καὶ **ἐλθόντες** εἰς τὴν οἰκίαν εἶδον τὸ παιδίον μετὰ
  and **having-come** into the house they-saw the child   with

  Μαρίας τῆς μητρὸς αὐτοῦ
  Mary   the mother of-him

  (Matthew 2.11)

ἐλθόντες is aorist.

RECOGNIZING PARTICIPLES

As we have seen, the correct translation of a participle based on tense, voice, gender, case and number is necessary to correctly interpret some of the ambiguities of the Greek New Testament. The tense of a participle tells us when the action is taking place and the number, gender and case tell us who the participle is referring to.

Like verbs, we recognize participles by their additions, inserts and endings. However, there are so many possible variations that a participle can have that it would not be helpful to list them all here. What follows is a list of general characteristics and trends that may help you to recognize some of the most common features.

1 Number, gender and case.

- Many masculine and neuter active participles have ...ντ... in the ending (e.g. πιστευο**ντ**α, πιστευσα**ντ**ων).

- Many feminine active participles have ...ασ... in the ending (e.g. πιστευου**ασ**α, πιστευσ**ασ**αις).

- Many passive participles of any gender have ...μεν... in the ending (e.g. πιστευο**μεν**ου, πιστευα**μεν**ης).

- Participles use a variety of endings to mark cases (nominative, accusative, genitive, dative). Some follow λογος and δοξα, but others follow the more irregular third declension nouns. The only easy one to spot is the genitive plural which always ends in ων

2 Tense

- Like aorist subjunctives, imperatives and infinitives, aorist participles have no additions to the beginning of the stem; instead the aorist tense is marked by the insertion of σ between the stem and ending in the active voice (e.g. πιστευω becomes πιστευ**σ**ας) and θ in the passive voice (e.g. πιστευ**θ**εις).

- Perfect participles do have an addition as well as an insert. They have the first letter of the stem plus ε at the beginning of the stem and κ as an insert in the active (e.g. πιστευω becomes **πε**πιστευ**κ**ως). In the passive, they just have the addition at the beginning (e.g. **πε**πιστευμενος).

- When a verb has an irregular past tense (e.g. ἔρχομαι which becomes ἦλθον in the aorist) the same stem is used to form the participle but without the addition. So the aorist participle of this verb is ἐλθών.

You will notice quickly from the examples that follow just how varied the endings of the participle are. In general, aim simply at being able to recognize that something is a participle and attempt to work out from the context (and meaning) which word(s) each participle goes with. If you need to know exactly what the form is you will have to check it on a website or similar resource.

Practice with Participles

Study the following sentences with the participles marked in bold and see if you can recognize some of the patterns that have been pointed out to you. Finally, when you are clear about the meanings of the words, try putting the sentences into good English.[3]

1 Ὃς δ' ἂν   σκανδαλίσῃ   ἕνα τῶν μικρῶν

whoever might-cause-to-stumble one of-the   little   (ones)

τούτων τῶν **πιστευόντων** εἰς ἐμέ,

these the-(ones) **believing**   into me

(Matthew 18.6)

πιστευόντων is a genitive masculine plural present active participle.

2 Καὶ αὐτοὶ **προσκυνήσαντες** αὐτὸν ὑπέστρεψαν εἰς

and they **having-worshipped** him they-returned into

Ἰερουσαλὴμ μετὰ χαρᾶς μεγάλης

Jerusalem with great joy

(Luke 24.52)

προσκυνήσαντες is a nominative masculine plural aorist active participle.

3 καὶ πάντες οἱ   **ἀκούσαντες** ἐθαύμασαν περὶ τῶν

and all the-(ones) **having-heard** were-amazed about the

λαληθέντων   ὑπὸ τῶν ποιμένων πρὸς αὐτούς·

(things)-having-been-spoken by the shepherds to   them

(Luke 2.18)

ἀκούσαντες is a nominative masculine plural aorist active participle.

λαληθέντων is a genitive neuter plural aorist passive participle.

4 καὶ πᾶς   ὁ **ἀκούων** μου τοὺς λόγους τούτους καὶ μὴ

and every the-one **hearing** my the words these and not

ποιῶν αὐτοὺς

doing them

(Matthew 7.26)

ἀκούων and ποιῶν are both nominative masculine singular present active participles.

TRANSLATING GREEK PARTICIPLES

Adding Words in the English

In general, when we translate Greek into English, we make a compromise between a word-for-word translation and something that reads well. This becomes particularly clear when participles are used as adverbs, as you have probably noticed. In our translations of the Greek in the section above, we had to supply additional words to make the English make sense. This can be a real challenge when translating participles, because Greek uses them much more often than English. For example, we wouldn't often say something like 'Having had a cup of tea, I walked down to the shops'. Instead we might say 'After I'd had a cup of tea, I walked down to the shops'.

As noted on pp. 178–9, the 'strict sense' of the Greek is best given in English by particular words and endings. We often translate the present active participle with '...ing' (e.g. 'believing'), the present passive participle with 'being ...ed' (e.g. 'being believed'), the past active participle with 'having ...ed' (e.g. 'having believed') and the past passive participle with 'having been ...ed' (e.g. 'having been believed'). However, you will often have to add in extra words to make the English make more sense: words like 'who', 'which', 'as', 'when', 'once', etc.

Take a look at this sentence. It has three participles in it, and each gives us some important information:

Καὶ **παράγων**   ὁ Ἰησοῦς ἐκεῖθεν εἶδεν ἄνθρωπον

and **passing-by** the   Jesus from-there he-saw   a-man

καθήμενον ἐπὶ τὸ τελώνιον, Μαθθαῖον **λεγόμενον**, καὶ

sitting   at the tax-booth, Matthew **being-called**, and

λέγει αὐτῷ·

he-said to-him

(Matthew 9.9)

The three participles have been highlighted in bold both in English and Greek to help you see what role they have in the sentence.

- The first participle tells us something more about Jesus – he was passing by.

- The second participle tells us something more about 'a man' that Jesus saw – he was sitting at a tax-booth.

- The third participle also tells us something more about 'a man' that Jesus saw – people called him Matthew.

If you were to try turning the Greek sentence above into a single sentence of readable English, you might end up with something like this:

> *As* Jesus was passing by, he saw a man *who was* sitting at a tax booth *and whose* name was Matthew.

Long Greek Sentences

Take a look at that sentence again. In order to make it into good English we might split it into several sentences, adding extra words if necessary. So in English it might look something like this:

> Jesus was passing by. He saw a man who was sitting at a tax booth. The man was called Matthew

We do this because in English short sentences are regarded as a good thing. If you use a computer, its grammar-checking facility will often tell you off if you use long sentences!

In Greek, however, long sentences are regarded as a good thing and they are often formed by adding one participle after another. Paul is particularly famous for this: some of his sentences seem to go on for ever; they can therefore be very difficult to put into good clear English.

Look at the following example from Romans 1.1–7:

Παῦλος δοῦλος Χριστοῦ Ἰησοῦ, κλητὸς ἀπόστολος

Paul   slave of-Christ Jesus   called   apostle

ἀφωρισμένος   εἰς εὐαγγέλιον θεοῦ,   ὃ

having-been-set-apart into   Gospel   of-God which

προεπηγγείλατο   διὰ   τῶν προφητῶν αὐτοῦ ἐν

he-promised-beforehand through the   prophets of-him in

γραφαῖς ἁγίαις περὶ τοῦ υἱοῦ αὐτοῦ τοῦ

writings   holy about the son of-him the-one

γενομένου   ἐκ σπέρματος Δαυὶδ   κατὰ

having-come-into-being from   seed   of David according-to

σάρκα, τοῦ   **ὁρισθέντος**   υἱοῦ θεοῦ ἐν

flesh, the-one **having-been-marked-off** as son of-God in

δυνάμει   κατὰ πνεῦμα ἁγιωσύνης ἐξ ἀναστάσεως

power according-to spirit of-holiness out-of resurrection

νεκρῶν, Ἰησοῦ Χριστοῦ τοῦ κυρίου ἡμῶν,   δι᾽ οὗ

of-the-dead Jesus   Christ   the Lord   of-us through whom

ἐλάβομεν χάριν καὶ ἀποστολὴν εἰς ὑπακοὴν

we-received grace and apostleship into endurance

πίστεως ἐν πᾶσιν τοῖς ἔθνεσιν   ὑπὲρ   τοῦ ὀνόματος

of-faith in   all   the nations on-behalf-of the   name

αὐτοῦ, ἐν οἷς   ἐστε   καὶ ὑμεῖς κλητοὶ Ἰησοῦ Χριστοῦ,

of-him in whom you-are also you   called of-Jesus Christ

πᾶσιν τοῖς **οὖσιν** ἐν Ῥώμη ἀγαπητοῖς θεοῦ, κλητοῖς

to-all those **being** in Rome   beloved of-God called

ἁγίοις, χάρις ὑμῖν καὶ εἰρήνη ἀπὸ θεοῦ πατρὸς ἡμῶν

holy   grace to-you and peace from God   Father of-us

καὶ κυρίου Ἰησοῦ Χριστοῦ.

and Lord   Jesus   Christ

Believe it or not, this is all a single sentence. The participles are all marked in bold: look at them to see how Paul uses participles to extend the sentence. Also notice that he uses other words to do this as well, particularly prepositions (such as 'through', 'in', etc.) and relative pronouns ('who', 'which', etc.). One of the challenges when trying to make sense of Paul is to work out how his long sentences work and to try to put them into as clear an English sentence structure as possible. Spend some time looking at these verses and see if you can make sense of what Paul is talking about here (your English translations might prove useful). How might you rewrite this in readable English? You might want to refer to some English versions of the New Testament to get some ideas.

SPECIAL USES OF THE PARTICIPLE IN THE GREEK NEW TESTAMENT

λεγων, λέγοντες

In Hebrew when someone is about to speak, the word 'saying' is often inserted before their words almost as speech marks.

This is often reproduced in the Greek New Testament with the participle λεγων (singular) or λέγοντες (plural) which means 'saying', from the verb λεγω, 'I say'. They are usually in the nominative case, because it's usually the subject of the sentence or phrase who is speaking. For example:

καὶ ἰδοὺ   ἔκραξαν λέγοντες·

and behold they-cried-out saying

(Matthew 8.29)

ἀπεκρίθη αὐτοῖς ὁ Ἰωάννης λέγων· ἐγὼ βαπτίζω ἐν ὕδατι·

answered to-them   John   saying 'I   baptize in water'

(John 1.26)

Each time you see this, you will need to decide how to translate it. Quite often, it may be best to miss it out entirely.

The Genitive Absolute

We have noticed already that participles go with the nouns they describe and match the function that the noun has in the sentence. Have a look at the following sentence in which this is the case:

ὑμῖν πρῶτον **ἀναστήσας**   ὁ θεὸς τὸν παῖδα αὐτοῦ

to-you first   **having-raised** the God the child of-him

ἀπέστειλεν αὐτὸν **εὐλογοῦντα** ὑμᾶς

he-sent   him   **blessing**   you

(Acts 3.26)

The first participle, ἀναστήσας, is nominative. It tells us more about the subject of the sentence, God (he *raised* his child).

The second participle, εὐλογοῦντα, is accusative. It tells us more about the object of the sentence, God's child (he was sent blessing us or to bless us).

In each instance, the participle describes more about a noun *in the sentence*.

Occasionally, however, the author may want to tell us something about an event which is entirely unconnected with the rest of the sentence. Look at the following sentence:

καὶ **ὑστερήσαντος**   οἴνου λέγει ἡ μήτηρ τοῦ ᾽Ιησοῦ πρὸς

and **having-run-out** of-wine said the mother of   Jesus   to

αὐτόν·

him

(John 2.3)

Here the subject of the sentence (nominative) is the mother of Jesus and the object (accusative) is him (i.e. Jesus). However, the wine running out is connected neither to Jesus' mother nor to Jesus: it does not tell us more about either the subject or the object of the sentence.

When this happens, Greek puts the phrase entirely into the genitive to show that it is not connected to the subject or object of the sentence. Grammatically this is known as the **genitive absolute**. Knowing this will make little difference to how you translate a sentence, but if you see the term you will understand what it means.

THE ARTICULAR INFINITIVE

In Chapter 7 we encountered the infinitive, the form of the verb normally translated as 'to . . .' (e.g. 'to do'). The vast majority of infinitives that you come across in the New Testament will be translated like this, but there is a type of infinitive which has a slightly different meaning and it is worth looking at here. It is the **articular infinitive**, so called because it has a definite article in front of it. When it occurs in this form its meaning changes in one of two ways:

1 The infinitive may appear simply with a definite article before it. When this happens, it can either be translated as, for example, 'to do' or as a kind of abstract noun, for example, 'the doing'. Have a look at the following sentence:

ὁ δὲ θεὸς τῆς ὑπομονῆς καὶ τῆς παρακλήσεως

the but God of-endurance and of-encouragement

δῴη   ὑμῖν **τὸ** αὐτὸ **φρονεῖν** ἐν ἀλλήλοις·

may-he-give to-you **the** same **thinking** in one-another

κατα   Χριστὸν Ἰησοῦν,

according-to Christ   Jesus

(Romans 15.5)

τὸ αὐτο **φρονεῖν** could also be translated as 'to think the same'.
As with participles, you may have to work at your translation
to make the best sense of it in English.

2 The infinitive may appear with a definite article *and* a preposition before it.

- Preceded by the preposition διa, the phrase means 'because
  of . . .'. For example:

  διαπονούμενοι   **διa**   **τὸ διδάσκειν** αὐτοὺς τὸν λαὸν

  being-disturbed **because the teaching**   them   the people

  (Acts 4.2)

  This could be translated as 'being disturbed because of their
  teaching of the people'.

- Preceded by εἰς or προς, the phrase means 'in order that
  . . .' or 'so that . . .' For example:

  Μὴ   οὖν   βασιλευέτω ἡ ἁμαρτία ἐν τῷ θνητῷ ὑμῶν

  not therefore   let-it-rule the   sin   in the mortal of-you

  σώματι **εἰς**   **τὸ ὑπακούειν** ταῖς ἐπιθυμίαις αὐτοῦ,

  body **so-that the listening** to-the   desires   of-it

  (Romans 6.12)

This could be translated as 'Do not let sin rule in your mortal bodies so that you listen to its desires'.

This meaning (i.e. 'in order that' or 'so that') can also be indicated when the definite article is in the *genitive* and there is no preposition. For example:

του πιστευειν υμας means 'so that you believe'.

- Preceded by ἐν, the phrase means 'when . . .' or 'while . . .'. For example:

καὶ **ἐν τῷ σπείρειν** αὐτὸν

and **in the sowing**   him

(Matthew 13.4)

This could be translated as 'while he sowed'.

- Preceded by μετα, the phrase means 'after . . .' For example:

καὶ παρέστησεν ἑαυτὸν ζῶντα **μετὰ τὸ   παθεῖν** αὐτὸν

and he-presented himself   living **after   the suffering** him

(Acts 1.3)

This could be translated 'and he presented himself alive after he had suffered'.

- Preceded by προ, the phrase means 'before . . .'

Πρὸ   τοῦ δὲ   **ἐλθεῖν** τὴν πίστιν

before the but **coming**   the   faith

(Galatians 3.23)

This could be translated 'before faith came'.

In short, when an infinitive occurs with the definite article and a preposition it has a meaning which is not always entirely obvious. Your task here is to attempt to put the sentence into English that makes sense, and it will often feel as though you have to change the meaning significantly in order to do this.

LOOKING AT TRANSLATIONS

Look at the following text:

ἐπειδήπερ   πολλοὶ ἐπεχείρησαν   ἀνατάξασθαι

inasmuch-as   many have-attempted to-arrange-in-order

διήγησιν   περὶ τῶν **πεπληροφορημένων** ἐν ἡμῖν

a-narrative about the   having-been-fulfilled in   us

πραγμάτων, καθὼς   παρέδοσαν   ἡμῖν οἱ ἀπ᾽ ἀρχῆς

deeds   just-as they-handed-over to-us the from beginning

αὐτόπται καὶ ὑπηρέται **γενόμενοι** τοῦ λόγου,

eyewitnesses and   servants   being   of-the word

ἔδοξε   κἀμοὶ **παρηκολουθηκότι**   ἄνωθεν

it-seemed also-to-me   in-following   from-the-start/above

πᾶσιν   ἀκριβῶς   καθεξῆς   σοι γράψαι, κράτιστε

everything accurately successively to-you to-write,   noble

Θεόφιλε, ἵνα   ἐπιγνῷς   περὶ ὧν

Theophilus so-that you-might-know about what

κατηχήθης   λόγων τὴν ἀσφάλειαν.

you-have-heard words the   certainty

(Luke 1.1–4)

Pay particular attention to the participles (marked in bold) and ask yourself how they have been translated by each of the translations given below:

Many have undertaken to draw up an account of the things that have been fulfilled among us, just as they were handed down to us by those who from the first were eyewitnesses and servants of the word. Therefore, since I myself have carefully investigated everything from the beginning, it seemed good also to me to write an orderly account for you, most excellent Theophilus, so that you may know the certainty of the things you have been taught. (NIV)

Dear Theophilus: Many people have done their best to write a report of the things that have taken place among us. They wrote what we have been told by those who saw these things from the beginning and who proclaimed the message. And so, your Excellency, because I have carefully studied all these matters from their beginning, I thought it would be good to write an orderly account for you. I do this so that you will know the full truth about everything which you have been taught. (GNB)

Inasmuch as many have taken in hand to set in order a narrative of those things which have been fulfilled among us, just as those who from the beginning were eyewitnesses and ministers of the word delivered them to us, it seemed good to me also, having had perfect understanding of all things from the very first, to write to you an orderly account, most excellent Theophilus, that you may know the certainty of those things in which you were instructed. (NKJV)

REVIEW OF LEARNING

In this chapter we have looked at:

• participles: their characteristics and uses;

• recognizing and translating participles;

• special uses of the participle: λεγων, λεγοντες and the genitive absolute;

• the articular infinitive.

Notes

1 In the NRSV, these passages are translated as follows: . . . Jesus turned to them and said, (Luke 23.28); When he was abused, he did not return abuse (1 Peter 2.23); . . . and heard them arguing with one another (Mark 12.28); the events that have been fulfilled among us (Luke 1.1).

2 You may find it difficult to turn these into readable English! A translation preserving the meaning of the tense of the participle might be something like this: (1) And having heard (this), the disciples fell on their faces and were greatly afraid; (2) As he saw the mighty wind, he was afraid; (3) Having come into the house, they saw the child with Mary, his mother

3 (1) whoever might cause one of these little ones believing in me to stumble; (2) And having worshipped him they returned to Jerusalem with great joy; (3) And all those having heard were amazed by the things having been spoken to them by the shepherds; (4) and everyone hearing these words of mine and not doing them.

Epilogue

It is often said that the more you know the more you realize you don't know: by now you should have a keen sense of what you don't know! Nevertheless, if you have read through this book carefully you should have gained some real insights into the way the language works, the subtleties of the Greek text which are often lost in translation, and the sorts of dilemmas facing translators of the New Testament into English. By making use of the Internet and/or published resources, you should be in a position to explore the Greek New Testament for yourself, raising your own questions and enriching your Bible study. The knack is to recognize how much you still have to learn, and yet to be bold about making use of what you have already learnt. To guide your future study, here are some 'Don'ts' and 'Dos':

1 **Don't worry about what you can't do.** There will be parts of the New Testament that you simply cannot translate. You need to be aware of this and not allow it to distress you. Be pleased with what you can do and don't worry about what you can't do, as what you can do will increase with practice anyway.

2 **Don't feel you need to know everything.** This course has attempted to teach you the rudiments of Greek and how to make relatively little knowledge go a long way with 'inspired guesswork'. There will be times when you feel overwhelmed by the complexities of the language. It's a normal reaction – don't let it put you off exploring for yourself.

3 **Don't be too dogmatic about what you learn from the Greek.** What the Greek means is often heavily disputed even by 'experts'. Any basic introduction to Greek sometimes has to simplify complex issues in order to make its point. This book has given you a sense of what *usually* happens in Greek, but there are always exceptions. Don't let what you know blind you to the complexity of it all.

4 **Do go back over what we have done.** Once through Greek grammar is rarely enough – there is no shame in doing it again (and again), so go back over the bits you haven't grasped yet. Rather than just relying on the examples given in the text, make use of the websites and the published works you have been introduced to in order to do a bit of 'exploring' of your own.

5 **Do use your Greek regularly.** Language learning is a bit like learning a musical instrument – you only get joy out of it when you have practised hard. So make it a discipline to use the Greek text regularly (at least once a week if you intend to improve). Look at different translations of passages as often as you can, picking a passage that interests you and comparing them to see how different translators have interpreted the text. If you are in a context where you hear the New Testament read out on a regular basis then take your inter-linear with you and follow the reading in the Greek as much as you can.

6 **Do go on and learn more Greek.** If you have enjoyed what you have done, go on and do more. You may like to use a more formal grammar like W.D. Mounce's *Basics of Biblical Greek* (Zondervan, 1993), or join a formal Greek study group. What you have done so far will give you a bit of help as you begin more study.

But whatever you do – enjoy it! The learning of Greek should enrich your reading of the New Testament and open up some possibilities you hadn't thought of before. We hope that this course has given you enough insights to whet your appetite, and start you on a lifelong journey of exploration.

A Check List of Grammatical Words used in this Course

Accusative used of nouns, the grammatical term used when a noun is the object of a verb
e.g. God created *the world*.

Active used of verbs, voice, denotes that the subject does the action
e.g. God *created* the world.

Adjective a word used to describe a noun further
e.g. A *good* book.

Adverb a word used to describe a verb further
e.g. He ran *quickly*.

Aorist used of verbs, a tense which describes a single action in the past
e.g. She freed the slave.

Article there are two kinds of article: the definite article (*the*) and the indefinite article (*a*). In Greek there is a word for the definite article but no word for the indefinite article.

Conjunction a word that joins sentences, clauses or words together
e.g. *and*, *but*, *because*

Dative used of nouns, the grammatical term used when a noun is the indirect object of the verb
e.g. He gave the book *to him*.

Declension	used of nouns and adjectives, the family or type of noun to which a word belongs
Definite article	the word '*the*'
Feminine	describes the gender of nouns, adjectives, pronouns and participles
Future	used of verbs, a tense which describes action in the future e.g. She will go home.
Gender	in Greek all nouns, adjectives, pronouns and participles have a gender (masculine, feminine or neuter). In the case of people the gender they have is obvious (e.g. woman is feminine) but 'things' are less obvious (e.g. word is masculine).
Genitive	used of nouns, the grammatical term used for possession e.g. The mother *of the girl* or *the girl's* mother.
Imperative	used of verbs, mood, a command e.g. *Go*
Imperfect	used of verbs, tense, incomplete action in the past e.g. He was reading his book, or he used to read his book
Indefinite article	the word '*a*' (there is no word for this in Greek)
Indicative	used of verbs, mood, makes a statement or asks a question (the normal verb)
Indirect object	used of nouns, in grammatical terms it is called the dative e.g. He gave the book *to him*.

Infinitive	used of verbs, mood, describes general action without reference to particular person or thing, normally prefaced by 'to' e.g. *to sit, to stand*
Masculine	describes the gender of nouns, adjectives, pronouns and participles.
Mood	used of verbs, describes the manner of action i.e. statement, command, indefinite, etc. . . . (indicative, imperative, infinite, subjunctive, participle)
Neuter	describes the gender of nouns, adjectives, pronouns and participles
Nominative	used of nouns, the grammatical term used for the subject of the verb e.g. *God* created the world.
Noun	the name of a person or thing e.g. *table, woman, God, Jane*
Number	used of many different parts of speech, singular or plural
Object	used of nouns, in grammatical terms it is called the accusative. It is the person or thing on which the verb is done. e.g. God created *the world.*
Parse	the term used to describe splitting up a sentence by identifying different parts of speech, i.e. noun, verb, etc.
Participle	used of verbs, mood, normally translated with '...ing', e.g. *sitting, running.* A participle is a verbal adjective, as a verb it is a doing word; as an adjective it describes the noun in more detail. e.g. Jesus, *loving* the disciples, said to them . . .

Passive   used of verbs, voice, denotes that the action
                     is done to the subject
                     e.g. the world *is created* by God.

Perfect   used of verbs, a tense which describes an
                     action in the past which affects the present,
                     often translated in English with 'has' or
                     'have'
                     e.g. The woman *has freed* the slave (and
                     hence the slave is now free).

Person   used of verbs, describes who is doing the
                     verb (first person = I, we; second person =
                     you, third person = he, she, it or they)

Pluperfect   used of verbs, a tense, most commonly used
                     in indirect speech, which describes action
                     further back in the past than the occasion
                     described, often translated in English as
                     'had'
                     e.g. I said to him that I *had read* the book.

Possessive   used of nouns, in grammatical terms it is
                     called the genitive. It is the person or thing to
                     which an object belongs.
                     e.g. The mother *of the girl* or *the girl's*
                     mother

Preposition   a word used to denote the location of a noun
                     (in, on, to, by, before, etc. . . .)
                     e.g. The book was *on* the table.

Present   used of verbs, a tense, used to describe action
                     currently taking place
                     e.g. The boy *is running* away or The boy
                     runs away.

Pronoun   a word used instead of a noun
                     e.g. I, you, they, he, etc. . . .

Subject	used of nouns, in grammatical terms it is called the nominative. It is the person or thing that does the verb. e.g. *God* created the world.
Subjunctive	used of verbs, mood, expresses a thought or wish and implies uncertainty, in English often translated with might e.g. I *might come* tomorrow.
Tense	used of verbs, to describe *when* an action takes or took place, (present, past or future)
Verb	a doing word which describes action of some sort
Vocative	used of nouns, the grammatical term used for people or objects being addressed, often translated in English with 'O' e.g. O *God*, may your name be hallowed.
Voice	used of verbs to describe whether the subject does the action or is acted upon

Appendix: Useful Tables

Table A1 Prepositions and their endings (chapter 2)

Preposition	with accusative	with genitive	with dative
ἀπο		out of	
ἀρχι		until	
εἰς	into		
ἐκ		out of	
ἐν			in, on
ἐπι	on	on	on
ἐξω		outside of	
ἑως		until	
δια	because of	through	
κατα	according to	against	
μετα	after	with	
ὀπισω		after	
παρα	to beside	from, from beside	(rest) beside, with
περι	about	about	
προ		before	
προς	towards		
ὑπερ	above	on behalf of	
ὑπο	under	by	
συν			with
χωρι		apart from	

Table A2 The Definite Article (Chapter 4)

Singular			
	Masculine	**Feminine**	**Neuter**
Nominative	ὁ	ἡ	το
Accusative	τον	την	το
Genitive	του	της	του
Dative	τῳ	τῃ	τῳ
Plural			
Nominative	οἱ	αἱ	τα
Accusative	τους	τας	τα
Genitive	των	των	των
Dative	τοις	ταις	τοις

Table A3   Nouns (Chapters 4 and 5)

	Like the Masculine Definite Article	Like the Feminine and Neuter Definite Articles			
		Singular			
Nominative	λογος	ἀρχη	καρδια	δοξα	ἐργον
Accusative	λογον	ἀρχην	καρδιαν	δοξαν	ἐργον
Genitive	λογου	ἀρχης	καρδιας	δοξης	ἐργου
Dative	λογῳ	ἀρχῃ	καρδιᾳ	δοξῃ	ἐργῳ
		Plural			
Nominative	λογοι	ἀρχαι	καρδιαι	δοξαι	ἐργα
Accusative	λογους	ἀρχας	καρδιας	δοξας	ἐργα
Genitive	λογοων	ἀρχων	καρδιων	δοξων	ἐργων
Dative	λογοις	ἀρχαις	καρδιαις	δοξαις	ἐργοις

Table A4   Nouns that are not like any of the definite articles

	Singular						
Nominative	ἀστηρ	πατηρ	σωμα	γενος	ἰχθυς	πολις	βασιλευς
Accusative	ἀστερα	πατερα	σωμα	γενος	ἰχθυν	πολιν	βασιλεα
Genitive	ἀστερος	πατρος	σωματος	γενους	ἰχθυος	πολεως	βασιλεως
Dative	ἀστερι	πατρι	σωματι	γενει	ἰχθυι	πολει	βασιλει

	Plural						
Nominative	ἀστερες	πατερες	σωματα	γενη	ἰχθυες	πολεις	βασιλεις
Accusative	ἀστερας	πατερας	σωματα	γενη	ἰχθυας	πολεις	βασιλεις
Genitive	ἀστερων	πατερων	σωματων	γενων	ἰχθυων	πολεων	βασιλεων
Dative	ἀστεροιν	πατρασιν	σωμασιν	γενεσιν	ἰχθυσιν	πολεσιν	βασιλευσιν

Table A5   Personal Pronouns: 1st and 2nd Person (Chapter 5)

	1st Person Singular	Meaning	2nd Person Singular	Meaning
Nominative	ἐγω	I	συ	you
Accusative	ἐμε (με)	me	σε	you
Genitive	ἐμου (μου)	my	σου	your
Dative	ἐμοι (μοι)	to me	σοι	to you

	1st Person Plural	Meaning	2nd Person Plural	Meaning
Nominative	ἡμεις	we	ὑμεις	you
Accusative	ἡμας	us	ὑμας	you
Genitive	ἡμων	our	ὑμων	your
Dative	ἡμιν	to us	ὑμιν	to you

Table A6   Personal Pronouns: 3rd Person (Chapter 5)

Singular			
Nominative	αὐτος	αὐτη	αὐτο	he / she / it
Accusative	αὐτον	αὐτην	αὐτο	him / her / it
Genitive	αὐτου	αυτῆς	αὐτου	his / hers / its
Dative	αὐτῳ	αὐτη	αὐτῳ	to him / to her / to it
Plural			
Nominative	αὐτοι	αὐται	αὐτα	they
Accusative	αὐτους	αὐτας	αὐτα	them
Genitive	αὐτων	αὐτων	αὐτων	theirs
Dative	αὐτοις	αὐταις	αὐτοις	to them

Table A7   Endings for Most Adjectives (Chapter 6)

	Masculine	Feminine	Neuter
Singular			
Nominative	κακος	κακη	κακον
Accusative	κακον	κακην	κακον
Genitive	κακου	κακης	κακου
Dative	κακῳ	κακῃ	κακῳ
Plural			
Nominative	κακοι	κακαι	κακα
Accusative	κακους	κακας	κακα
Genitive	κακων	κακων	κακων
Dative	κακοις	κακαις	κακοις

Table A8   An unusual and important adjective (each, every, all)

	Masculine	Feminine	Neuter
Singular			
Nominative	πας	πασα	παν
Accusative	παντα	πασαν	παν
Genitive	παντος	πασης	παντος
Dative	παντι	παση	παντι
Plural			
Nominative	παντες	πασαι	παντα
Accusative	παντας	πασας	παντα
Genitive	παντων	πασων	παντων
Dative	πασι	πασαις	πασι

Table A9   Demonstratives: 'That' (Chapter 6)

	Masculine	Feminine	Neuter
Singular			
Nominative	ἐκεινος	ἐκεινη	ἐκεινο
Accusative	ἐκεινον	ἐκεινην	ἐκεινο
Genitive	ἐκεινου	ἐκεινης	ἐκεινου
Dative	ἐκεινῳ	ἐκεινῃ	ἐκεινῳ
Plural			
Nominative	ἐκεινοι	ἐκειναι	ἐκεινα
Accusative	ἐκεινους	ἐκεινας	ἐκεινα
Genitive	ἐκεινων	ἐκεινων	ἐκεινων
Dative	ἐκεινοις	ἐκειναις	ἐκεινοις

Table A10   Demonstratives: 'This' (Chapter 6)

	Masculine	Feminine	Neuter
Singular			
Nominative	οὗτος	αὕτη	τουτο
Accusative	τουτον	ταυτην	τουτο
Genitive	τουτου	ταυτης	τουτων
Dative	τουτῳ	ταυτη	τουτῳ
Plural			
Nominative	οὗτοι	αὗται	ταυτα
Accusative	τουτους	ταυτας	ταυτα
Genitive	τουτων	ταυτων	τουτων
Dative	τουτοις	ταυταις	τουτοις

Table A11   Simple Present Verbs (Chapter 7)

Form of Word	Meaning		Ending
λεγω	I say	1st Person Singular	- ω
λεγεις	You say	2nd Person Singular	- εις
λεγει	He, She it says	3rd Person Singular	- ει
λεγομεν	We say	1st Person Plural	- ομεν
λεγετε	You say	2nd Person Plural	- ετε
λεγουσιν	They say	3rd Person Plural	- ουσιν

Table A12　A full chart of εἰμι

Person	Present	Future	Imperfect	Subjunctive	Infinitive	Participle
1 singular	εἰμι	ἐσομαι	ἠμην	ὠ	εἰναι	ὢν (masc.)
						οὐσα (fem.)
						ὀν (neut.)
2 singular	εἶ	ἐσῃ	ἠς (or ἠσθα)	ῃς		
3 singular	ἐστιν	ἐσται	ἠν	ᾐ		
1 plural	ἐσμεν	ἐσομεθα	ἠμεν (or ἠμεθα)ν	ὠμε		
2 plural	ἐστε	ἐσεσθε	ἠτε	ῃτε		
3 plural	εἰσιν	εσονται	ἠσαν	ὠσιν		

Table A13 The most common μι verb δίδωμι – I give

	Person	Present Active	Aorist Active	Aorist Passive
Indicative	1 sing.	διδωμι	ἐδωκα	ἐδοθην
	2 sing.	διδως	ἐδωκας	ἐδοθης
	3 sing.	διδωσι	ἐδωκε(ν)	ἐδοθη
	1 plural	διδομεν	ἐδωκαμεν	ἐδοθημεν
	2 plural	διδοτε	ἐδωκατε	ἐδοθητε
	3 plural	διδοασι	ἐδωκαν	ἐδοθησαν
Subjunctive	1 sing.	διδω	δω	δοθω
	2 sing.	διδῳς	δῳς	δοθης
	3 sing.	διδῳ	δῳ	δοθη
	1 plural	διδωμεν	δωμεν	δοθωμεν
	2 plural	διδωτε	δωτε	δοθητε
	3 plural	διδωσι	δωσι	δοθωσι
Imperative	2 sing.	διδου	δος	δοθητι
	3 sing.	διδοτω	δοτω	δοθητω
	2 plural	διδοτε	δοτε	δοθητε
	3 plural	διδοτωσαν	δοτωσαν	δοθητωσαν
Infinitive		διδοναι	δουναι	δοθηναι
Participle	Masc.	διδους	δους	δοθεις
	Fem.	διδουσα	δουσα	δοθεισα
	Neut.	διδον	δον	δοθεν

Table A14   Active Indicative Tenses

Person	Present	Future	Imperfect	Aorist	Perfect
1st sing.	πιστεύω	πιστεύσω	ἐπίστευον	ἐπίστευσα	λεπιστευκα
2nd sing.	πιστεύεις	πιστεύσεις	ἐπίστευες	ἐπίστευσας	λεπιστευκας
3rd sing.	πιστεύει	πιστεύσει	ἐπίστευε(ν)	ἐπίστευσε(ν)	λεπιστευκε(ν)
1st plural	πιστεύομεν	πιστεύσομεν	ἐπιστεύομεν	ἐπιστεύσαμεν	λεπιστευκαμεν
2nd plural	πιστεύετε	πιστεύσετε	ἐπιστεύετε	ἐπιστεύσατε	λεπιστευκατε
3rd plural	πιστεύουσι(ν)	πιστεύσουσι(ν)	ἐπίστευον	ἐπίστευσαν	λεπιστευκασι(ν)

Table A15   Active Subjunctives

Person	Present		Aorist	
1st sing.	πιστεύω		πιστεύσω	
2nd sing.	πιστεύης		πιστεύσης	
3rd sing.	πιστεύη		πιστεύση	
1st plural	πιστεύωμεν		πιστεύσωμεν	
2nd plural	πιστεύητε		πιστεύσητε	
3rd plural	πιστεύωσιν		πιστεύσωσιν	

Table A16   Active Imperatives

Person	Present		Aorist	
1st sing.				
2nd sing.	πιστευε		πιστευσον	
3rd sing.	πιστευετω		πιστευσατω	
1st plural				
2nd plural	πιστευετε		πιστευσατε	
3rd plural	πιστευετωσαν		πιστευσωσαν	

Table A17   Active Infinitives

Person	Present		Aorist	Perfect
	πιστευειν		πιστευσαι	πεπιστευκεναι

Table A18   Passive Indicative Tenses

Person	Present Passive	Future Passive	Imperfect Passive	Aorist Passive	Perfect Passive
1st sing.	πιστευομαι	πιστευθησομαι	ἐπιστευομην	ἐπιστευθην	πεπιστευμαι
2nd sing.	πιστευη	πιστευθηση	ἐπιστευου	ἐπιστευθης	πεπιστευσαι
3rd sing.	πιστευεται	πιστευθησεται	ἐπιστευετο	ἐπιστευθη	πεπιστευται
1st plural	πιστευομεθα	πιστευθησομεθα	ἐπιστευομεθα	ἐπιστευθημεν	πεπιστευμεθα
2nd plural	πιστευεσθε	πιστευθησεσθε	ἐπιστευεσθε	ἐπιστευθητε	πεπιστευσθε
3rd plural	πιστευονται	πιστευθησονται	ἐπιστευοντο	ἐπιστευθησαν	πεπιστευνται

Table A19   Passive Subjunctives

Person	Present	Aorist
1st sing.	πιστευωμαι	πιστευθω
2nd sing.	πιστευη	πιστευθης
3rd sing.	πιστευηται	πιστευθη
1st plural	πιστευωμεθα	πιστευθωμεν
2nd plural	πιστευησθε	πιστευθητε
3rd plural	πιστευωνται	πιστευθωσιν

Table A20   Passive Imperatives

Person	Present	Aorist
1st sing.		
2nd sing.	πιστευου	πιστευθητι
3rd sing.	πιστευεσθω	πιστευθητω
1st plural		
2nd plural	πιστευεσθε	πιστευθητε
3rd plural	πιστευεσθωσαν	πιστευθητωσαν

Table A21   Passive Infinitives

Person	Present	Aorist	Perfect
	πιστευεσθαι	πιστευθηναι	πεπιστευσθαι

Table A22   Middle Indicative (or normal) tenses

Person	*Present Middle	Future Middle	*Imperfect Middle	Aorist Middle	*Perfect Middle
1st sing.	πιστευομαι	πιστευσομαι	ἐπιστευομην	ἐπιστευσαμην	πεπιστευμαι
2nd sing.	πιστευη	πιστευση	ἐπιστευου	ἐπιστευσω	πεπιστευσαι
3rd sing.	πιστευεται	πιστευσεται	ἐπιστευετο	ἐπιστευσατο	πεπιστευται
1st plural	πιστευομεθα	πιστευσομεθα	ἐπιστευομεθα	ἐπιστευσαμεθα	πεπιστευμεθα
2nd plural	πιστευεσθε	πιστευσεσθε	ἐπιστευεσθε	ἐπιστευσασθε	πεπιστευσθε
3rd plural	πιστευονται	πιστευσονται	ἐπιστευοντο	ἐπιστευσαντο	πεπιστευνται

Columns marked * are exactly the same as the Passive, only the Future and Aorist forms are different from the passive.

Table A23   Middle Subjunctives

Person	*Present	Aorist
1st sing.	πιστευωμαι	πιστευσωμαι
2nd sing.	πιστευη	πιστευση
3rd sing.	πιστευηται	πιστευσηται
1st plural	πιστευωμεθα	πιστευσωμεθα
2nd plural	πιστευησθε	πιστευσησθε
3rd plural	πιστευωνται	πιστευσωνται

Columns marked * are exactly the same as the Passive, only the Future and Aorist forms are different from the passive.

Table A24 Middle Imperatives

Person	*Present	Aorist
1st sing.		
2nd sing.	πιστευου	πιστευσαι
3rd sing.	πιστευεσθω	πιστευσασθω
1st plural		
2nd plural	πιστευεσθε	πιστευσασθε
3rd plural	πιστευεσθωσαν	πιστευσασθωσα

Columns marked * are exactly the same as the Passive, only the Future and Aorist forms are different from the passive.

Table A25 Middle Infinitives

Person	Present	Aorist	*Perfect
	πιστευεσθαι	πιστευσαι	πεπιστευσθαι

Columns marked * are exactly the same as the Passive, only the Future and Aorist forms are different from the passive.

Lexicon of Greek Words

This list contains all the words (apart from proper names) that appear more than a hundred times in the New Testament, along with the most important ones that appear in the examples in the rest of this book. For the sake of simplicity, all accents have been omitted except breathing marks. We have given only one English translation for most words, but you will soon discover that some Greek words can be translated in a variety of ways! You will need to look at a more comprehensive lexicon or a website in order to gain an understanding of the range of meanings each word covers.

ἀγαθος, -η, -ον	good
ἀγαπαω	I love
ἀγαπη, -ης (f.)	love
ἀγιος, -α, -ον	holy
ἀγγελος, -ου (m.)	angel, messenger
ἀγω	I lead
ἀδελφος, -ου (m.)	brother
αἰρω	I pick up
αἰων, -ωνος (m.)	age
ἀκαστασια, -ας (f.)	insurrection
ἀκουω	I hear
ἀληθεια, -ας (f.)	truth
ἀλλα	but

ἀλλος, -η, -ο	other
ἀμαρτια, -ας (f.)	sin
ἀμαρτωλος, ον (m.)	sinful
ἀμην	Amen
ἀν	(usually not translated)
ἀναστασις, -εως (f.)	resurrection
ἀνηρ, ἀνδρος (m.)	man
ἀνθρωπος, -ου (m.)	person
ἀνιστημι	I arise
ἀπερχομαι	I go away
ἀπο	(with gen.) from
ἀποθνησκω	I die
ἀποκρινομαι	I answer
ἀπολλυμι	I destroy
ἀποστελλω	I send
ἀρτος, -ου (m.)	bread
ἀρχαιος, -α, -ον	old
ἀρχη, ης (f.)	beginning, at first
ἀρχιερευς, -εως (m.)	chief priest
ἀρχομαι	I begin
ἀρχω	I rule
ἀρχων, -οντος (m.)	ruler
ἀστηρ, -ερος (m.)	star
ἀτυος, -η, -ο	he, she, it
ἀφιημι	I forgive
ἀφοβως	without fear
βαλλω	I throw
βαπτιζω	I baptize
βασιλεια, -ας (f.)	kingdom
βασιλειος, -ον	royal
βασιλευς, -εως (m.)	king

βασιλευω	I rule
βασιλικος, -η, -ον	royal, kingly
βασιλισσα, -ης (f.)	queen
βλεπω	I see
γαρ	for
γενος, -ους (n.)	nation
γη, γης (f.)	earth
γινομαι	I become
γινωσκω	I know
γραφω	I write
γυνη, -αικος (f.)	woman
δε	but, and
δει	it is necessary
δια	(with acc.) because of (with gen.) through
διαβολος, -ου (m.)	devil
διδωμι	I give
δικαιος, -α, -ον	righteous
δικαιοω	I treat as righteous
δοξα, -ης (f.)	glory
δουλος, -ου (m.)	servant
δυναμαι	I am able
δυναμις, -εως (f.)	power
δυναμοω	I strengthen
δυναστης, -ου (m.)	ruler
δυνατος, -η, -ον	strong
δυο	two
ἐαν	if
ἑαυτου, -ης, -ου	himself/herself/itself
ἐγειρω	I raise up
ἐγω	I

ἔθνος, -ους (n.)	nation
εἰ	if
εἰμι	I am
εἰπεν	he/she/it said
εἰρηνη, -ης (f.)	peace
εἰρηνικος, -η, -ον	peaceful
εἰρηνοποιεω	I make peace
εἰς	(with acc.) into
εἰς, μια, ἐν	one
εἰσερχομαι	I come in
ἐκ, ἐξ	(with gen.) out of
ἐκει	there
ἐκεινος, -η, -ο	that one
ἐκκλεσια, -ας (f.)	assembly
ἐκστασις, -εως (f.)	amazement
ἐλεος, -ους (n.)	mercy
ἐλπιζω	I hope
ἐν	in
ἐξερχομαι	I go out
ἐξουσια, -ας (f.)	authority
ἐξω	outside
ἐπι	(with acc./gen./dat.) on
ἐργαζομαι	I work
ἐργον, -ου (n.)	work
ἐρχομαι	I come
ἐρωταω	I ask
ἐσθιω	I eat
ἐσχατως	finally
εὐθεως	immediately
εὐλογητος, -η, -ον	praised
εὑρισκω	I find

ἐχω	I have
ἑως	until
ζαω (or ζω)	I am alive
ζητεω	I seek
ζωη, -ης (f.)	life
ἡ	or
ἡμεις	we
ἡμερα, -ας (f.)	day
θανατος, -ου (m.)	death
θελω	I wish
θεος, -ου (m.)	God
θεραπευω	I heal
θυσια, -ας (f.)	sacrifice
ἰδιος, -α, -ον	alone
ἰδου	See!
ἰερατευμα, -ατος (n.)	priesthood
ἰερατευω	serve as a priest
ἰερος, -α, -ον	holy
ἰνα	in order that
ἰστημι	I stand
ἰσχυω	I am able
ἰχθυς, -υος (m.)	fish
καγω	I also
καθευδω	I sleep
καθως	just as
και	and
κακος, -η, -ον	evil
καλεω	I call
καλος, -η, ον	good
καλως	rightly
καρδια, -ας (f.)	heart

καρπος, -ου (m.)	fruit
κατα	(with acc.) according to (with gen.) against
καταργεω	I nullify
κοπτω	I cut, lament
κοσμος, -ου (m.)	world
κρινω	I judge
κυριος, -ου (m.)	Lord
λαλεω	I speak
λαμβανω	I receive
λαος, -ου (m.)	people
λεγω	I say
λογος, -ου (m.)	word
λυω	I loose
μαθητης, -ου (m.)	disciple
μανθανω	I discover
μαστιγοω	I whip
μεγας, -αλη, -α	great
μελλω	I am about to
μεν	either/or, 'on the one hand'
μενω	I stay
μετα	(with acc.) after (with gen.) with
μη	not
μηδε	and not
μηδεις, -εμια, -εν	no one
μηδεποτε	never
μηδεπω, μηπω	not yet
μηκετι	no longer
μονος, -η, -ον	only
μου (ἐμου)	my

νεκρος, -α, -ον	dead
νομος, -ου (m.)	law
νυν	now
ὁ, ἡ, το	the
ὁδος, -ου (f.)	road
οἰδα	I know
οἰκος, -ου (m.)	house
ὁλος, -η, -ον	whole
ὁμοιως	similarly
ὀνομα, -ατος (n.)	name
ὁραω	I see
ὁριον, -ου	region
ὁς, ἡ, ὁ	who
ὁσος, -η, -ον	as much/many as
ὁστις, ἡτις, ὁ τι	whoever/whatever
ὁταν	whenever
ὁτε	when
ὁτι	because
οὐ, οὐκ, οὐχ, οὐχι	not
οὐδε, οὐτε	and not
οὐδεις, -εμια, -εν	no one, nothing
οὐδεποτε	never
οὐδεπω, οὐπω	not yet
οὐκετι	no longer
οὐν	therefore
οὐρανος, -ου (m.)	sky
οὑτος, αὑτη, τουτο	this
οὑτως	thus
ὀφθαλμος, -ου (m.)	eye
ὀχλος, -ου (m.)	crowd
παιδιον, -ου (n.)	child

παλιν	again
παρα	(with acc.) alongside (with gen.) from (with dat.) beside
παραδιδωμι	I hand over
παρακαλεω	I beg
παραμενω	I stay
παραχειμαζω	I spend the winter
πας, πασα, παν	all
πατηρ, πατρος (m.)	father
πεμπω	I appoint
περι	(with acc) concerning (with gen.) about
πιστευω	I believe
πιστις, -εως (f.)	faith
πνευμα, -ατος (n.)	spirit
ποιεω	I do
πολεμος, -ου (m.)	war
πολις, -εως (f.)	city
πολυς, πολλη, πολυ	many
πορευομαι	I go
προ	(with gen.) before
προπεμπω	I send
προς	(with acc.) toward
προσεχω	I watch out for
προφητης, -ου (m.)	prophet
πρωτος, -η, -ον	first
πτοεομαι	I am terrified
πως	how?
σαρξ, σαρκος (f.)	flesh
σταυροω	I crucify

συ	you
συζαω	I live with somebody
συν	with
συναγωγη, -ης (f.)	synagogue
συνεδριον, -ου (n.)	council
σωζω	I save
σωμα, σωματος (n.)	body
τε	and
τελος	end
τιθημι	I put
τις, τι	who/what?
τοτε	then
τυπτω	I beat
υἱος, -ου (m.)	son
ὑμεις	you (pl.)
ὑπερ	(with acc.) above (with gen.) on behalf of
ὑπο	(with acc.) under (with gen.) by
ὑποστασις, -εως (f.)	confidence
φωνη, -ης (f.)	sound
χαρις, χαριτος (f.)	grace
χειρ, χειρος (f.)	hand
Χριστος, -ου (m.)	Christ
ψυχη, -ης (f.)	mind
ὡρα, -ας (f.)	hour
ὡς	as